Mastering Machine Learning with scikit-learn

Second Edition

Learn to implement and evaluate machine learning solutions
with scikit-learn

Gavin Hackeling

BIRMINGHAM - MUMBAI

Mastering Machine Learning with scikit-learn

Second Edition

First published: October 2014

second published: July 2017

Production reference: 1200717

Published by Packt Publishing Ltd.
Livery Place
35 Livery Street
Birmingham
B3 2PB, UK.
ISBN 978-1-78829-987-9

www.packtpub.com

Credits

Author
Gavin Hackeling

Reviewer
Oleg Okun

Commissioning Editor
Amey Varangaonkar

Acquisition Editor
Aman Singh

Content Development Editor
Aishwarya Pandere

Technical Editor
Suwarna Patil

Copy Editors
Safis Editing
Vikrant Phadkay

Project Coordinator
Nidhi Joshi

Proofreader
Safis Editing

Indexer
Tejal Daruwale Soni

Graphics
Tania Dutta

Production Coordinator
Arvindkumar Gupta

About the Author

Gavin Hackeling is a data scientist and author. He was worked on a variety of machine learning problems, including automatic speech recognition, document classification, object recognition, and semantic segmentation. An alumnus of the University of North Carolina and New York University, he lives in Brooklyn with his wife and cat.

I would like to thank my wife, Hallie, and the scikti-learn community.

About the Reviewer

Oleg Okun is a machine learning expert and an author/editor of four books, numerous journal articles, and conference papers. His career spans more than a quarter of a century. He was employed in both academia and industry in his motherland, Belarus, and abroad (Finland, Sweden, and Germany). His work experience includes document image analysis, fingerprint biometrics, bioinformatics, online/offline marketing analytics, credit scoring analytics, and text analytics.

He is interested in all aspects of distributed machine learning and the Internet of Things. Oleg currently lives and works in Hamburg, Germany.

> *I would like to express my deepest gratitude to my parents for everything that they have done for me.*

www.PacktPub.com

For support files and downloads related to your book, please visit www.PacktPub.com.

Did you know that Packt offers eBook versions of every book published, with PDF and ePub files available? You can upgrade to the eBook version at www.PacktPub.com and as a print book customer, you are entitled to a discount on the eBook copy. Get in touch with us at service@packtpub.com for more details.

At www.PacktPub.com, you can also read a collection of free technical articles, sign up for a range of free newsletters and receive exclusive discounts and offers on Packt books and eBooks.

https://www.packtpub.com/mapt

Get the most in-demand software skills with Mapt. Mapt gives you full access to all Packt books and video courses, as well as industry-leading tools to help you plan your personal development and advance your career.

Why subscribe?

- Fully searchable across every book published by Packt
- Copy and paste, print, and bookmark content
- On demand and accessible via a web browser

Customer Feedback

Thanks for purchasing this Packt book. At Packt, quality is at the heart of our editorial process. To help us improve, please leave us an honest review on this book's Amazon page at `https://www.amazon.com/dp/1788299876`.

If you'd like to join our team of regular reviewers, you can e-mail us at `customerreviews@packtpub.com`. We award our regular reviewers with free eBooks and videos in exchange for their valuable feedback. Help us be relentless in improving our products!

Table of Contents

Preface

In recent years, popular imagination has become fascinated by machine learning. The discipline has found a variety of applications. Some of these applications, such as spam filtering, are ubiquitous and have been rendered mundane by their successes. Many other applications have only recently been conceived, and hint at machine learning's potential.

In this book, we will examine several machine learning models and learning algorithms. We will discuss tasks that machine learning is commonly applied to, and we will learn to measure the performance of machine learning systems. We will work with a popular library for the Python programming language called scikit-learn, which has assembled state-of-the-art implementations of many machine learning algorithms under an intuitive and versatile API.

What this book covers

Chapter 1, *The Fundamentals of Machine Learning*, defines machine learning as the study and design of programs that improve their performance of a task by learning from experience. This definition guides the other chapters; in each, we will examine a machine learning model, apply it to a task, and measure its performance.

Chapter 2, *Simple Linear Regression*, discusses a model that relates a single feature to a continuous response variable. We will learn about cost functions and use the normal equation to optimize the model.

Chapter 3, *Classification and Regression with K-Nearest Neighbors*, introduces a simple, nonlinear model for classification and regression tasks.

Chapter 4, *Feature Extraction*, describes methods for representing text, images, and categorical variables as features that can be used in machine learning models.

Chapter 5, *From Simple Linear Regression to Multiple Linear Regression*, discusses a generalization of simple linear regression that regresses a continuous response variable onto multiple features.

Chapter 6, *From Linear Regression to Logistic Regression*, further generalizes multiple linear regression and introduces a model for binary classification tasks.

Chapter 7, *Naive Bayes*, discusses Bayes' theorem and the Naive Bayes family of classifiers, and compares generative and discriminative models.

Chapter 8, *Nonlinear Classification and Regression with Decision Trees*, introduces the decision tree, a simple, nonlinear model for classification and regression tasks.

Chapter 9, *From Decision Trees to Random Forests and other Ensemble Methods*, discusses three methods for combining models called bagging, boosting, and stacking.

Chapter 10, *The Perceptron*, introduces a simple online model for binary classification.

Chapter 11, *From the Perceptron to Support Vector Machines*, discusses a powerful, discriminative model for classification and regression called the support vector machine, and a technique for efficiently projecting features to higher dimensional spaces.

Chapter 12, *From the Perceptron to Artificial Neural Networks*, introduces powerful nonlinear models for classification and regression built from graphs of artificial neurons.

Chapter 13, *K-means*, discusses an algorithm that can be used to find structures in unlabeled data.

Chapter 14, *Dimensionality Reduction with Principal Component Analysis*, describes a method for reducing the dimensions of data that can mitigate the curse of dimensionality.

What you need for this book

The examples in this book require Python >= 2.7 or >= 3.3 and pip, the PyPA recommended tool for installing Python packages. The examples are intended to be executed in a Jupyter notebook or an IPython interpreter. Chapter 1, *The Fundamentals of Machine Learning* shows how to install scikit-learn 0.18.1, its dependencies, and other libraries on Ubuntu, Mac OS, and Windows.

Who this book is for

This book is intended for software engineers who want to understand how common machine learning algorithms work and develop an intuition for how to use them. It is also for data scientists who want to learn about the scikit-learn API. Familiarity with machine learning fundamentals and Python is helpful but not required.

Conventions

In this book, you will find a number of text styles that distinguish between different kinds of information. Here are some examples of these styles and an explanation of their meaning.

Code words in text, database table names, folder names, filenames, file extensions, pathnames, dummy URLs, user input, and Twitter handles are shown as follows: "The package is named `sklearn` because scikit-learn is not a valid Python package name."

```
# In[1]:
import sklearn
sklearn.__version__

# Out[1]:
'0.18.1'
```

New terms and **important words** are shown in bold.

 Warnings or important notes appear like this.

 Tips and tricks appear like this.

Reader feedback

Feedback from our readers is always welcome. Let us know what you thought about this book-what you liked or disliked. Reader feedback is important for us as it helps us to develop titles that you will really get the most out of. To send us general feedback, simply email feedback@packtpub.com, and mention the book's title in the subject of your message. If there is a topic that you have expertise in and you are interested in either writing or contributing to a book, see our author guide at www.packtpub.com/authors.

Customer support

Now that you are the proud owner of a Packt book, we have a number of things to help you to get the most from your purchase.

Downloading the example code

You can download the example code files for this book from your account at `http://www.packtpub.com`. If you purchased this book elsewhere, you can visit `http://www.packtpub.com/support` and register to have the files e-mailed directly to you. You can download the code files by following these steps:

1. Log in or register to our website using your e-mail address and password.
2. Hover the mouse pointer on the **SUPPORT** tab at the top.
3. Click on **Code Downloads & Errata**.
4. Enter the name of the book in the **Search** box.
5. Select the book for which you're looking to download the code files.
6. Choose from the drop-down menu where you purchased this book from.
7. Click on **Code Download**.

Once the file is downloaded, please make sure that you unzip or extract the folder using the latest version of:

- WinRAR / 7-Zip for Windows
- Zipeg / iZip / UnRarX for Mac
- 7-Zip / PeaZip for Linux

The code bundle for the book is also hosted on GitHub at `https://github.com/PacktPublishing/Mastering-Machine-Learning-with-scikit-learn-Second-Edition`. We also have other code bundles from our rich catalog of books and videos available at `https://github.com/PacktPublishing/`. Check them out!

Errata

Although we have taken care to ensure the accuracy of our content, mistakes do happen. If you find a mistake in one of our books-maybe a mistake in the text or the code-we would be grateful if you could report this to us. By doing so, you can save other readers from frustration and help us to improve subsequent versions of this book. If you find any errata, please report them by visiting `http://www.packtpub.com/submit-errata`, selecting your book, clicking on the **Errata Submission Form** link, and entering the details of your errata. Once your errata are verified, your submission will be accepted and the errata will be uploaded to our website or added to any list of existing errata under the Errata section of that title. To view the previously submitted errata, go to `https://www.packtpub.com/books/content/support`and enter the name of the book in the search field. The required information will appear under the **Errata** section.

Piracy

Piracy of copyrighted material on the Internet is an ongoing problem across all media. At Packt, we take the protection of our copyright and licenses very seriously. If you come across any illegal copies of our works in any form on the Internet, please provide us with the location address or website name immediately. Please contact us at `copyright@packtpub.com` with a link to the suspected pirated material. We appreciate your help in protecting our authors and our ability to bring you valuable content.

Questions

If you have a problem with any aspects of this book, you can contact us at `questions@packtpub.com`, and we will do our best to address it.

1

The Fundamentals of Machine Learning

In this chapter, we will review fundamental concepts in machine learning. We will compare supervised and unsupervised learning; discuss the uses of training, testing, and validation data; and describe applications of machine learning. Finally, we will introduce scikit-learn, and install the tools required in subsequent chapters.

Defining machine learning

Our imaginations have long been captivated by visions of machines that can learn and imitate human intelligence. While machines capable of general artificial intelligence-like Arthur C. Clarke's HAL and Isaac Asimov's Sonny-have yet to be realized, software programs that can acquire new knowledge and skills through experience are becoming increasingly common. We use such machine learning programs to discover new music that we might enjoy, and to find exactly the shoes we want to purchase online. Machine learning programs allow us to dictate commands to our smart phones, and allow our thermostats to set their own temperatures. Machine learning programs can decipher sloppily-written mailing addresses better than humans, and can guard credit cards from fraud more vigilantly. From investigating new medicines to estimating the page views for versions of a headline, machine learning software is becoming central to many industries. Machine learning has even encroached on activities that have long been considered uniquely human, such as writing the sports column recapping the Duke basketball team's loss to UNC.

Machine learning is the design and study of software artifacts that use past experience to inform future decisions; machine learning is the study of programs that learn from data. The fundamental goal of machine learning is to generalize, or to induce an unknown rule from examples of the rule's application. The canonical example of machine learning is spam filtering. By observing thousands of emails that have been previously labeled as either spam or ham, spam filters learn to classify new messages. Arthur Samuel, a computer scientist who pioneered the study of artificial intelligence, said that machine learning is the "study that gives computers the ability to learn without being explicitly programmed". Throughout the 1950s and 1960s, Samuel developed programs that played checkers. While the rules of checkers are simple, complex strategies are required to defeat skilled opponents. Samuel never explicitly programmed these strategies, but through the experience of playing thousands of games, the program learned complex behaviors that allowed it to beat many human opponents.

A popular quote from computer scientist Tom Mitchell defines machine learning more formally: "A program can be said to learn from experience 'E' with respect to some class of tasks 'T' and performance measure 'P', if its performance at tasks in 'T', as measured by 'P', improves with experience 'E'." For example, assume that you have a collection of pictures. Each picture depicts either a dog or a cat. A task could be sorting the pictures into separate collections of dog and cat photos. A program could learn to perform this task by observing pictures that have already been sorted, and it could evaluate its performance by calculating the percentage of correctly classified pictures.

We will use Mitchell's definition of machine learning to organize this chapter. First, we will discuss types of experience, including supervised learning and unsupervised learning. Next, we will discuss common tasks that can be performed by machine learning systems. Finally, we will discuss performance measures that can be used to assess machine learning systems.

Learning from experience

Machine learning systems are often described as learning from experience either with or without supervision from humans. In **supervised learning** problems, a program predicts an output for an input by learning from pairs of labeled inputs and outputs. That is, the program learns from examples of the "right answers". In unsupervised learning, a program does not learn from labeled data. Instead, it attempts to discover patterns in data. For example, assume that you have collected data describing the heights and weights of people. An example of an unsupervised learning problem is dividing the data points into groups. A program might produce groups that correspond to men and women, or children and adults. Now assume that the data is also labeled with the person's sex. An example of a supervised learning problem is to induce a rule for predicting whether a person is male or female based on his or her height and weight. We will discuss algorithms and examples of supervised and unsupervised learning in the following chapters.

Supervised learning and unsupervised learning can be thought of as occupying opposite ends of a spectrum. Some types of problem, called **semi-supervised** learning problems, make use of both supervised and unsupervised data; these problems are located on the spectrum between supervised and unsupervised learning. **Reinforcement learning** is located near the supervised end of the spectrum. Unlike supervised learning, reinforcement learning programs do not learn from labeled pairs of inputs and outputs. Instead, they receive feedback for their decisions, but errors are not explicitly corrected. For example, a reinforcement learning program that is learning to play a side-scrolling video game like *Super Mario Bros* may receive a reward when it completes a level or exceeds a certain score, and a punishment when it loses a life. However, this supervised feedback is not associated with specific decisions to run, avoid Goombas, or pick up fire flowers. We will focus primarily on supervised and unsupervised learning, as these categories include most common machine learning problems. In the next sections, we will review supervised and unsupervised learning in more detail.

A supervised learning program learns from labeled examples of the outputs that should be produced for an input. There are many names for the output of a machine learning program. Several disciplines converge in machine learning, and many of those disciplines use their own terminology. In this book, we will refer to the output as the **response variable**. Other names for response variables include "dependent variables", "regressands", "criterion variables", "measured variables", "responding variables", "explained variables", "outcome variables", "experimental variables", "labels", and "output variables". Similarly, the input variables have several names. In this book, we will refer to inputs as features, and the phenomena they represent as **explanatory variables**. Other names for explanatory variables include "predictors", "regressors", "controlled variables", and "exposure variables". Response variables and explanatory variables may take real or discrete values.

The collection of examples that comprise supervised experience is called a **training set**. A collection of examples that is used to assess the performance of a program is called a **test set**. The response variable can be thought of as the answer to the question posed by the explanatory variables; supervised learning problems learn from a collection of answers to different questions. That is, supervised learning programs are provided with the **correct answers** and must learn to respond correctly to unseen, but similar, questions.

Machine learning tasks

Two of the most common supervised machine learning tasks are **classification** and **regression**. In classification tasks, the program must learn to predict discrete values for one or more response variables from one or more features. That is, the program must predict the most probable category, class, or label for new observations. Applications of classification include predicting whether a stock's price will rise or fall, or deciding whether a news article belongs to the politics or leisure sections. In regression problems, the program must predict the values of one more or continuous response variables from one or more features. Examples of regression problems include predicting the sales revenue for a new product, or predicting the salary for a job based on its description. Like classification, regression problems require supervised learning.

A common unsupervised learning task is to discover groups of related observations, called **clusters**, within the dataset. This task, called **clustering** or cluster analysis, assigns observations into groups such that observations within a groups are more similar to each other based on some similarity measure than they are to observations in other groups. Clustering is often used to explore a dataset. For example, given a collection of movie reviews, a clustering algorithm might discover the sets of positive and negative reviews. The system will not be able to label the clusters as **positive** or **negative**; without supervision, it will only have knowledge that the grouped observations are similar to each other by some measure. A common application of clustering is discovering segments of customers within a market for a product. By understanding what attributes are common to particular groups of customers, marketers can decide what aspects of their campaigns to emphasize. Clustering is also used by internet radio services; given a collection of songs, a clustering algorithm might be able to group the songs according to their genres. Using different similarity measures, the same clustering algorithm might group the songs by their keys, or by the instruments they contain.

Dimensionality reduction is another task that is commonly accomplished using unsupervised learning. Some problems may contain thousands or millions of features, which can be computationally costly to work with. Additionally, the program's ability to generalize may be reduced if some of the features capture noise or are irrelevant to the underlying relationship. Dimensionality reduction is the process of discovering the features that account for the greatest changes in the response variable. Dimensionality reduction can also be used to visualize data. It is easy to visualize a regression problem such as predicting the price of a home from its size; the size of the home can be plotted on the graph's x axis, and the price of the home can be plotted on the y axis. It is similarly easy to visualize the housing price regression problem when a second feature is added; the number of bathrooms in the house could be plotted on the z axis, for instance. A problem with thousands of features, however, becomes impossible to visualize.

Training data, testing data, and validation data

As mentioned previously, a training set is a collection of observations. These observations comprise the experience that the algorithm uses to learn. In supervised learning problems, each observation consists of an observed response variable and features of one or more observed explanatory variables. The test set is a similar collection of observations. The test set is used to evaluate the performance of the model using some performance metric. It is important that no observations from the training set are included in the test set. If the test set does contain examples from the training set, it will be difficult to assess whether the algorithm has learned to generalize from the training set or has simply memorized it. A program that generalizes well will be able to effectively perform a task with new data. In contrast, a program that memorizes the training data by learning an overly-complex model could predict the values of the response variable for the training set accurately, but will fail to predict the value of the response variable for new examples. Memorizing the training set is called **overfitting**. A program that memorizes its observations may not perform its task well, as it could memorize relations and structure that are coincidental in the training data. Balancing generalization and memorization is a problem common to many machine learning algorithms. In later chapters we will discuss **regularization**, which can be applied to many models to reduce over-fitting.

In addition to the training and test data, a third set of observations, called a **validation** or **hold-out set**, is sometimes required. The validation set is used to tune variables called **hyperparameters** that control how the algorithm learns from the training data. The program is still evaluated on the test set to provide an estimate of its performance in the real world. The validation set should not be used to estimate real-world performance because the program has been tuned to learn from the training data in a way that optimizes its score on the validation data; the program will not have this advantage in the real world.

It is common to partition a single set of supervised observations into training, validation, and test sets. There are no requirements for the sizes of the partitions, and they may vary according to the amount of data available. It is common to allocate between fifty and seventy-five percent of the data to the training set, ten to twenty-five percent of the data to the test set, and the remainder to the validation set.

Some training sets may contain only a few hundred observations; others may include millions. Inexpensive storage, increased network connectivity, and the ubiquity of sensor-packed smartphones have contributed to the contemporary state of big data, or training sets with millions or billions of examples. While this book will not work with datasets that require parallel processing on tens or hundreds of computers, the predictive power of many machine learning algorithms improves as the amount of training data increases. However, machine learning algorithms also follow the maxim "garbage in, garbage out". A student who studies for a test by reading a large, confusing textbook that contains many errors likely will not score better than a student who reads a short but well-written textbook. Similarly, an algorithm trained on a large collection of noisy, irrelevant, or incorrectly-labeled data will not perform better than an algorithm trained on a smaller set of data that is more representative of the problem in the real-world.

Many supervised training sets are prepared manually or by semi-automated processes. Creating a large collection of supervised data can be costly in some domains. Fortunately, several datasets are bundled with scikit-learn, allowing developers to focus on experimenting with models instead. During development, and particularly when training data is scarce, a practice called **cross-validation** can be used to train and validate a model on the same data. In cross-validation, the training data is partitioned. The model is trained using all but one of the partitions, and tested on the remaining partition. The partitions are then rotated several times so that the model is trained and evaluated on all of the data. The mean of the model's scores on each of the partitions is a better estimate of performance in the real world than an evaluation using a single training/testing split. The following diagram depicts cross validation with five partitions, or folds.

	A	B	C	D	E
Cross Validation Iteration 1	Test	Train	Train	Train	Train
Cross Validation Iteration 2	Train	Test	Train	Train	Train
Cross Validation Iteration 3	Train	Train	Test	Train	Train
Cross Validation Iteration 4	Train	Train	Train	Test	Train
Cross Validation Iteration 5	Train	Train	Train	Train	Test

The original dataset is partitioned into five subsets of equal size labeled **A** through **E**. Initially the model is trained on partitions **B** through **E**, and tested on partition **A**. In the next iteration, the model is trained on partitions **A, C, D**, and **E**, and tested on partition **B**. The partitions are rotated until models have been trained and tested on all of the partitions. Cross-validation provides a more accurate estimate of the model's performance than testing a single partition of the data.

Bias and variance

Many metrics can be used to measure whether or not a program is learning to perform its task more effectively. For supervised learning problems, many performance metrics measure the amount of prediction error. There are two fundamental causes of prediction error: a model's **bias**, and its **variance**. Assume that you have many training sets that are all unique, but equally representative of the population. A model with high bias will produce similar errors for an input regardless of the training set it used to learn; the model biases its own assumptions about the real relationship over the relationship demonstrated in the training data. A model with high variance, conversely, will produce different errors for an input depending on the training set that it used to learn. A model with high bias is inflexible, but a model with high variance may be so flexible that it models the noise in the training set. That is, a model with high variance over-fits the training data, while a model with high bias under-fits the training data. It can be helpful to visualize bias and variance as darts thrown at a dartboard. Each dart is analogous to a prediction, and is thrown by a model trained on a different dataset every time. A model with high bias but low variance will throw darts that will be tightly clustered, but could be far from the bulls-eye. A model with high bias and high variance will throw darts all over the board; the darts are far from the bulls-eye and from each other. A model with low bias and high variance will throw darts that could be poorly clustered but close to the bulls-eye. Finally, a model with low bias and low variance will throw darts that are tightly clustered around the bulls-eye.

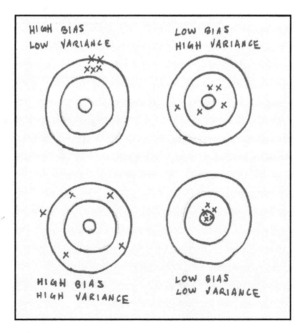

Ideally, a model will have both low bias and variance, but efforts to decrease one will frequently increase the other. This is known as the **bias-variance trade-off**. We will discuss the biases and variances of many of the models introduced in this book.

Unsupervised learning problems do not have an error signal to measure; instead, performance metrics for unsupervised learning problems measure some attribute of the structure discovered in the data, such as the distances within and between clusters.

Most performance measures can only be calculated for a specific type of task, like classification or regression. Machine learning systems should be evaluated using performance measures that represent the costs associated with making errors in the real world. While this may seem obvious, the following example describes this using a performance measure that is appropriate for the task in general but not for its specific application.

Consider a classification task in which a machine learning system observes tumors and must predict whether they are malignant or benign. Accuracy, or the fraction of instances that were classified correctly, is an intuitive measure of the program's performance. While accuracy does measure the program's performance, it does not differentiate between malignant tumors that were classified as being benign, and benign tumors that were classified as being malignant. In some applications, the costs associated with all types of errors may be the same. In this problem, however, failing to identify malignant tumors is likely a more severe error than mistakenly classifying benign tumors as being malignant.

We can measure each of the possible prediction outcomes to create different views of the classifier's performance. When the system correctly classifies a tumor as being malignant, the prediction is called a **true positive**. When the system incorrectly classifies a benign tumor as being malignant, the prediction is a **false positive**. Similarly, a **false negative** is an incorrect prediction that the tumor is benign, and a **true negative** is a correct prediction that a tumor is benign. Note that positive and negative are used only as binary labels, and are not meant to judge the phenomena they signify. In this example, it does not matter whether malignant tumors are coded as positive or negative, so long as they are coded consistently. True and false positives and negatives can be used to calculate several common measures of classification performance, including **accuracy**, **precision** and **recall**.

Accuracy is calculated with the following formula, where *TP* is the number of true positives, *TN* is the number of true negatives, *FP* is the number of false positives, and *FN* is the number of false negatives:

$$ACC = \frac{TP + TN}{TP + TN + FP + FN}$$

Precision is the fraction of the tumors that were predicted to be malignant that are actually malignant. Precision is calculated with the following formula:

$$P = \frac{TP}{TP + FP}$$

Recall is the fraction of malignant tumors that the system identified. Recall is calculated with the following formula:

$$R = \frac{TP}{TP + FN}$$

In this example, precision measures the fraction of tumors that were predicted to be malignant that are actually malignant. Recall measures the fraction of truly malignant tumors that were detected.

The precision and recall measures could reveal that a classifier with impressive accuracy actually fails to detect most of the malignant tumors. If most tumors in the testing set are benign, even a classifier that never predicts malignancy could have high accuracy. A different classifier with lower accuracy and higher recall might be better suited to the task, since it will detect more of the malignant tumors.

Many other performance measures for classification can be used. We will discuss more metrics, including metrics for multi-label classification problems, in later chapters. In the next chapter we will discuss some common performance measures for regression tasks. Performance on unsupervised tasks can also be assessed; we will discuss some performance measures for cluster analysis later in the book.

An introduction to scikit-learn

Since its release in 2007, scikit-learn has become one of the most popular machine learning libraries. scikit-learn provides algorithms for machine learning tasks including classification, regression, dimensionality reduction, and clustering. It also provides modules for pre-processing data, extracting features, optimizing hyperparameters, and evaluating models.

scikit-learn is built on the popular Python libraries NumPy and SciPy. NumPy extends Python to support efficient operations on large arrays and multi-dimensional matrices. SciPy provides modules for scientific computing. The visualization library matplotlib is often used in conjunction with scikit-learn.

scikit-learn is popular for academic research because its API is well-documented, easy-to-use, and versatile. Developers can use scikit-learn to experiment with different algorithms by changing only a few lines of code. scikit-learn wraps some popular implementations of machine learning algorithms, such as **LIBSVM** and **LIBLINEAR**. Other Python libraries, including NLTK, include wrappers for scikit-learn. scikit-learn also includes a variety of datasets, allowing developers to focus on algorithms rather than obtaining and cleaning data.

Licensed under the permissive BSD license, scikit-learn can be used in commercial applications without restrictions. Many of scikit-learn's algorithms are fast and scalable to all but massive datasets. Finally, scikit-learn is noted for its reliability; much of the library is covered by automated tests.

Installing scikit-learn

This book was written for version 0.18.1 of scikit-learn; use this version to ensure that the examples run correctly. If you have previously installed scikit-learn, you can retrieve the version number by executing the following in a notebook or Python interpreter:

```
# In[1]:
import sklearn
sklearn.__version__

# Out[1]:
'0.18.1'
```

> The package is named `sklearn` because scikit-learn is not a valid Python package name.

If you have not previously installed scikit-learn, you may install it from a package manager or build it from source. We will review the installation processes for Ubuntu 16.04, Max OS, and Windows 10 in the following sections, but refer to `http://scikit-learn.org/stable/install.html`for the latest instructions. The following instructions assume only that you have installed Python >= 2.6 or Python >= 3.3. See `http://www.python.org/download/` for instructions on installing Python.

Installing using pip

The easiest way to install scikit-learn is to use `pip`, the PyPA-recommended tool for installing Python packages. Install scikit-learn using `pip` as follows:

```
$ pip install -U scikit-learn
```

If pip is not available on your system, consult the following sections for installation instructions for various platforms.

Installing on Windows

scikit-learn requires setuptools, a third-party package that supports packaging and installing software for Python. Setuptools can be installed on Windows by running the bootstrap script at `https://bitbucket.org/pypa/setuptools/raw/bootstrap/ez_setup.py`.

Windows binaries for the 32-bit and 64-bit versions of scikit-learn are also available. If you cannot determine which version you need, install the 32-bit version. Both versions depend on NumPy 1.3 or newer. The 32-bit version of NumPy can be downloaded from `http://sourceforge.net/projects/numpy/files/NumPy/`. The 64-bit version can be downloaded from `http://www.lfd.uci.edu/~gohlke/pythonlibs/#scikit-learn`.

A Windows installer for the 32-bit version of scikit-learn can be downloaded from `http://sourceforge.net/projects/scikit-learn/files/`. An installer for the 64-bit version of scikit-learn can be downloaded from `http://www.lfd.uci.edu/~gohlke/pythonlibs/#scikit-learn`.

Installing on Ubuntu 16.04

scikit-learn can be installed on Ubuntu 16.04 using `apt`.

```
$ sudo apt install python-scikits-learn
```

Installing on Mac OS

scikit-learn can be installed on OS X using **Macports**.

```
$ sudo port install py27-sklearn
```

Installing Anaconda

Anaconda is a free collection of more than 720 open source data science packages for Python including scikit-learn, NumPy, SciPy, pandas, and matplotlib. Anaconda is platform-agnostic and simple to install. See `https://docs.continuum.io/anaconda/insta ll/` for instructions for your operating system.

Verifying the installation

To verify that scikit-learn has been installed correctly, open a Python console and execute the following:

```
# In[1]:
import sklearn
sklearn.__version__

# Out[1]:
'0.18.1'
```

To run scikit-learn's unit tests, first install the nose Python library. Then execute the following in a terminal emulator:

```
$ nosetest sklearn -exe
```

Congratulations! You've successfully installed scikit-learn.

Installing pandas, Pillow, NLTK, and matplotlib

pandas is an open source library that provides data structures and analysis tools for Python. pandas is a powerful library, and several books describe how to use pandas for data analysis. We will use a few of pandas's convenient tools for importing data and calculating summary statistics. Pillow is a fork of the Python Imaging Library, which provides a variety of image processing features. NLTK is a library for working with human language. As for scikit-learn, `pip` is the preferred installation method for pandas, Pillow, and NLTK. Execute the following command in a terminal emulator:

```
$ pip install pandas pillow nltk
```

Matplotlib is a library for easily creating plots, histograms, and other charts with Python. We will use it to visualize training data and models. Matplotlib has several dependencies. Like pandas, matplotlib depends on NumPy, which should already be installed. On Ubuntu 16.04, matplotlib and its dependencies can be installed with:

```
$ sudo apt install python-matplotlib
```

Binaries for Mac OS and Windows 10 can be downloaded from `http://matplotlib.org/d ownloads.html`.

Summary

In this chapter, we defined machine learning as the design of programs that can improve their performance at a task by learning from experience. We discussed the spectrum of supervision in experience. At one end is supervised learning, in which a program learns from inputs that are labeled with their corresponding outputs. Unsupervised learning, in which the program must discover structure in only unlabeled inputs, is at the opposite end of the spectrum. Semi-supervised approaches make use of both labeled and unlabeled training data.

Next we discussed common types of machine learning tasks and reviewed examples of each. In classification tasks the program predict the value of a discrete response variable from the observed explanatory variables. In regression tasks the program must predict the value of a continuous response variable from the explanatory variables. Unsupervised learning tasks include clustering, in which observations are organized into groups according to some similarity measure, and dimensionality reduction, which reduces a set of explanatory variables to a smaller set of synthetic features that retain as much information as possible. We also reviewed the bias-variance trade-off and discussed common performance measures for different machine learning tasks.

In this chapter we discussed the history, goals, and advantages of scikit-learn. Finally, we prepared our development environment by installing scikit-learn and other libraries that are commonly used in conjunction with it. In the next chapter we will discuss a simple model for regression tasks, and build our first machine learning model with scikit-learn.

2
Simple Linear Regression

In this chapter, we will introduce our first model, **simple linear regression**. Simple linear regression models the relationship between one response variable and one feature of an explanatory variable. We will discuss how to fit our model, and we will work through a toy problem. While simple linear regression is rarely applicable to real-world problems, understanding it is essential to understanding many other models. In subsequent chapters, we will learn about generalizations of simple linear regression and apply them to real-world datasets.

Simple linear regression

In the previous chapter, we learned that training data is used to estimate the parameters of a model in supervised learning problems. Observations of explanatory variables and their corresponding response variables comprise training data. The model can be used to predict the value of the response variable for values of the explanatory variable that have not been previously observed. Recall that the goal in regression problems is to predict the value of a continuous response variable. In this chapter, we will examine simple linear regression, which can be used to model a linear relationship between one response variable and one feature representing an explanatory variable.

Suppose you wish to know the price of a pizza. You might simply look at a menu. This, however, is a machine learning book, so instead we will use simple linear regression to predict the price of a pizza based on an attribute of the pizza that we can observe, or an explanatory variable. Let's model the relationship between the size of a pizza and its price. First, we will write a program with scikit-learn that can predict the price of a pizza given its size. Then we will discuss how simple linear regression works and how it can be generalized to work with other types of problems.

Let's assume that you have recorded the diameters and prices of pizzas that you have previously eaten in your pizza journal. These observations comprise our training data:

Training instance	Diameter in inches	Price in dollars
1	6	7
2	8	9
3	10	13
4	14	17.5
5	18	18

We can visualize our training data by plotting it on a graph using matplotlib:

```
# In[1]:
import numpy as np  # "np" and "plt" are common aliases for NumPy and
    Matplotlib, respectively.
import matplotlib.pyplot as plt

# X represents the features of our training data, the diameters of the
pizzas.
# A scikit-learn convention is to name the matrix of feature vectors X.
# Uppercase letters indicate matrices, and lowercase letters indicate
vectors.
X = np.array([[6], [8], [10], [14], [18]]).reshape(-1, 1)
y = [7, 9, 13, 17.5, 18]  # y is a vector representing the prices of
    the pizzas.

plt.figure()
plt.title('Pizza price plotted against diameter')
plt.xlabel('Diameter in inches')
plt.ylabel('Price in dollars')
plt.plot(X, y, 'k.')
plt.axis([0, 25, 0, 25])
plt.grid(True)
plt.show()
```

The comments in the script state that X represents a matrix of pizza diameters, and y represents a vector of pizza prices. The reasons for this decision will become clear in the next chapter. This script produces the following plot. The diameters of the pizzas are plotted on the *x* axis, and the prices are plotted on the *y* axis:

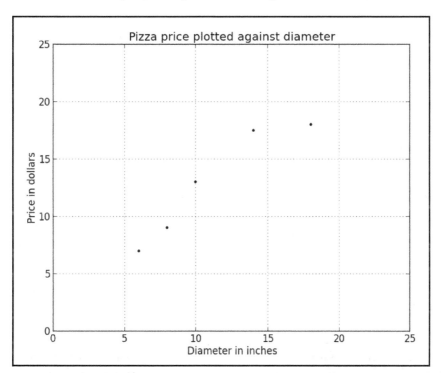

We can see from the plot of the training data that there is a positive relationship between the diameter of a pizza and its price, which should be corroborated by our own pizza-eating experience. As the diameter of a pizza increases, its price generally increases. The following pizza price predictor program models this relationship using simple linear regression. Let's review the program and discuss how simple linear regression works:

```
# In[2]:
from sklearn.linear_model import LinearRegression
model = LinearRegression()  # Create an instance of the estimator
model.fit(X, y)  # Fit the model on the training data

# Predict the price of a pizza with a diameter that has never been seen
before
test_pizza = np.array([[12]])
predicted_price = model.predict(test_pizza)[0]
print('A 12" pizza should cost: $%.2f' % predicted_price)
```

```
# Out[2]:
A 12" pizza should cost: $13.68
```

Simple linear regression assumes that a linear relationship exists between the response variable and the explanatory variable; it models this relationship with a linear surface called a **hyperplane**. A hyperplane is a subspace that has one dimension less than the ambient space that contains it. In simple linear regression, there is one dimension for the response variable and another dimension for the explanatory variable, for a total of two dimensions. The regression hyperplane thus has one dimension; a hyperplane with one dimension is a line.

The `LinearRegression` class is an **estimator**. Estimators predict a value based on observed data. In scikit-learn, all estimators implement the `fit` methods and `predict`. The former method is used to learn the parameters of a model, and the latter method is used to predict the value of a response variable for an explanatory variable using the learned parameters. It is easy to experiment with different models using scikit-learn because all estimators implement the `fit` and `predict` methods; trying new models can be as simple as changing one line of code. The `fit` method of `LinearRegression` learns the parameters of the following model for simple linear regression:

$$y = \alpha + \beta x$$

In the preceding formula, y is the predicted value of the response variable; in this example, it is the predicted price of the pizza. x is the explanatory variable. The intercept term α and the coefficient β are parameters of the model that are learned by the learning algorithm. The hyperplane plotted in the following figure models the relationship between the size of a pizza and its price. Using this model, we would expect the price of an 8" pizza to be about *$7.33* and the price of a 20" pizza to be *$18.75*.

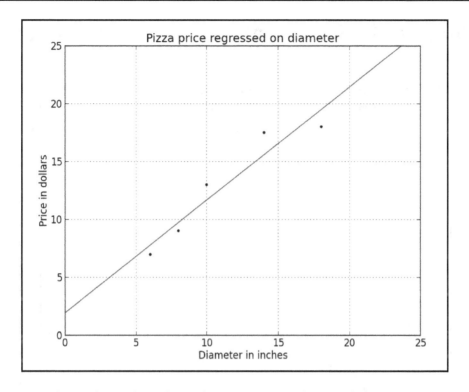

Using training data to learn the values of the parameters for simple linear regression that produce the best fitting model is called **ordinary least squares (OLS)** or **linear least squares**. In this chapter, we will discuss a method for analytically solving the values of the model's parameters. In subsequent chapters, we will learn approaches for approximating the values of parameters that are suitable for larger datasets. First, however, we must define what it means for a model to fit the training data.

Evaluating the fitness of the model with a cost function

Regression lines produced by several sets of parameter values are plotted in the following figure. How can we assess which parameters produced the best-fitting regression line?

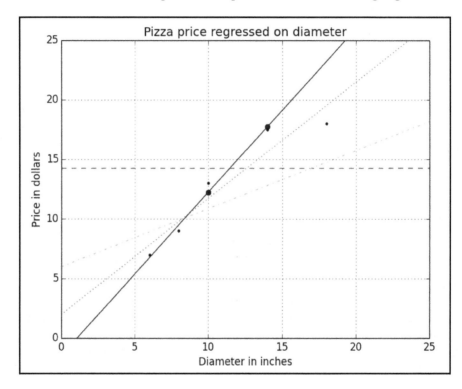

A **cost function**, also called a **loss function**, is used to define and measure the error of a model. The differences between the prices predicted by the model and the observed prices of the pizzas in the training set are called **residuals**, or **training errors**. Later, we will evaluate the model on a separate set of test data. The differences between the predicted and observed values in the test data are called **prediction errors**, or **test errors**. The residuals for our model are indicated by vertical lines between the points for the training instances and the regression hyperplane in the following plot:

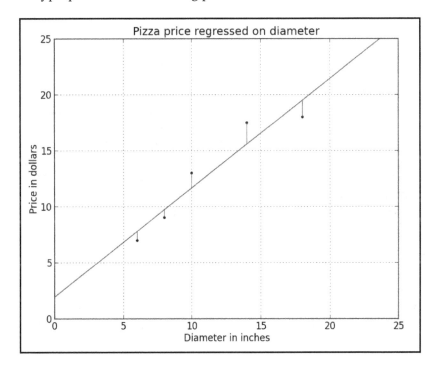

We can produce the best pizza-price predictor by minimizing the sum of the residuals. That is, our model fits if the values it predicts for the response variable are close to the observed values for all of the training examples. This measure of the model's fitness is called the **residual sum of squares (RSS)** cost function. Formally, this function assesses the fitness of a model by summing the squared residuals for all of our training examples. The RSS is calculated with the formula in the following equation, where y_i is the observed value and $f(x_i)$ is the predicted value:

$$SS_{res} = \sum_{i=1}^{n}(y_i - f(x_i))^2$$

Let's compute the RSS for our model by adding the following two lines to the previous script:

```
print('Residual sum of squares: %.2f' % np.mean((model.predict(X)
    - y) ** 2))
Residual sum of squares: 1.75
```

Now that we have a cost function, we can find the values of the model's parameters that minimize it.

Solving OLS for simple linear regression

In this section, we will work through solving OLS for simple linear regression. Recall that simple linear regression is given by the equation $y = \alpha + \beta x$ and that our goal is to solve for the values of β and α to minimize the cost function. We will solve for β first. To do so, we will calculate the **variance** of x and the **covariance** of x and y. Variance is a measure of how far a set of values are spread out. If all the numbers in the set are equal, the variance of the set is zero. A small variance indicates that the numbers are near the mean of the set, while a set containing numbers that are far from the mean and from each other will have a large variance. Variance can be calculated using the following equation:

$$var(x) = \frac{\sum_{i=1}^{n}(x_i - \bar{x})^2}{n-1}$$

$\bar{x}$ is the mean of x, x_i is the value of x for the ith training instance, and n is the number of training instances. Let's calculate `variance` of the pizza diameters in our training set:

```
# In[2]:
import numpy as np

X = np.array([[6], [8], [10], [14], [18]]).reshape(-1, 1)
x_bar = X.mean()
print(x_bar)

# Note that we subtract one from the number of training instances when
    calculating the sample variance.
# This technique is called Bessel's correction. It corrects the bias in the
estimation of the population variance
# from a sample.
variance = ((X - x_bar)**2).sum() / (X.shape[0] - 1)
print(variance)

# Out[2]:
```

```
11.2
23.2
```

NumPy also provides the method `var` for calculating variance. The keyword parameter `ddof` can be used to set Bessel's correction to calculate the sample variance:

```
# In[3]:
print(np.var(X, ddof=1))

# Out[3]:
23.2
```

Covariance is a measure of how much two variables change together. If the variables increase together, their covariance is positive. If one variable tends to increase while the other decreases, their covariance is negative. If there is no linear relationship between the two variables, their covariance will be equal to zero; they are linearly uncorrelated but not necessarily independent. Covariance can be calculated using the following formula:

$$cov(x, y) = \frac{\sum_{i=1}^{n}(x_i - \bar{x})(y_i - \bar{y})}{n - 1}$$

As with variance, x_i is the diameter of the ith training instance, $\bar{x}$ is the mean of the diameters, $\bar{y}$ is the mean of the prices, y_i is the price of the ith training instance, and n is the number of training instances. Let's calculate `covariance` of the diameters and prices of the pizzas in the training set:

```
# In[4]:
# We previously used a List to represent y.
# Here we switch to a NumPy ndarray, which provides a method to calulcate
the sample mean.
y = np.array([7, 9, 13, 17.5, 18])

y_bar = y.mean()
# We transpose X because both operands must be row vectors
covariance = np.multiply((X - x_bar).transpose(), y - y_bar).sum() /
  (X.shape[0] - 1)
print(covariance)
print(np.cov(X.transpose(), y)[0][1])

# Out[4]:
22.65
22.65
```

Now that we have calculated the variance of our explanatory variable and the covariance of the response and explanatory variables, we can solve for β using the following:

$$\beta = \frac{cov(x,y)}{var(x)}$$

$$\beta = \frac{22.65}{23.2} \approx 0.98$$

Having solved for β, we can solve for α using this formula:

$$\alpha = \bar{y} - \beta\bar{x}$$

Here, $\bar{y}$ is the mean of y and $\bar{x}$ is the mean of x. $(\bar{x}, \bar{y})$ are the coordinates of the centroid, a point that the model must pass through.

$$\alpha = 12.9 - 0.98 \times 11.2 \approx 1.97$$

Now that we have solved for the values of the model's parameters that minimize the cost function, we can plug in the diameters of the pizzas and predict their prices. For instance, an *11"* pizza should be expected to cost about *$12.70*, and an *18"* pizza should be expected to cost *$19.54*. Congratulations! You used simple linear regression to predict the price of a pizza.

Evaluating the model

We have used a learning algorithm to estimate a model's parameters from training data. How can we assess whether our model is a good representation of the real relationship? Let's assume that you have found another page in your pizza journal. We will use this page's entries as a test set to measure the performance of our model. We have added a fourth column; it contains the prices predicted by our model.

Test instance	Diameter in inches	Observed price in dollars	Predicted price in dollars
1	8	11	9.7759
2	9	8.5	10.7522
3	11	15	12.7048
4	16	18	17.5863

5	12	11	13.6811

Several measures can be used to assess our model's predictive capability. We will evaluate our pizza price predictor using a measure called **R-squared**. Also known as the **coefficient of determination**, R-squared measures how close the data are to a regression line. There are several methods for calculating R-squared. In the case of simple linear regression, R-squared is equal to the square of the **Pearson product-moment correlation coefficient (PPMCC)**, or **Pearson's r**. Using this method, R-squared must be a positive number between zero and one. This method is intuitive; if R-squared describes the proportion of variance in the response variable that is explained by the model, it cannot be greater than one or less than zero. Other methods, including the method used by scikit-learn, do not calculate R-squared as the square of Pearson's r. Using these methods, R-squared can be negative if the model performs extremely poorly. It is important to note the limitations of performance metrics. R-squared in particular is sensitive to outliers, and can spuriously increase when features are added to the model.

We will follow the method used by scikit-learn to calculate R-squared for our pizza price predictor. First we must measure the **total sum of squares**. y_i is the observed value of the response variable for the ith test instance, and $\bar{y}$ is the mean of the observed values of the response variable.

$$SS_{tot} = \sum_{i=1}^{n}(y_i - \bar{y})^2$$

$$SS_{tot} = (11 - 12.7)^2 + (8.5 - 12.7)^2 + \cdots + (11 - 12.7)^2 = 56.8$$

Next we must find the RSS. Recall that this is also our cost function.

$$SS_{res} = \sum_{i=1}^{n}(y_i - f(x_i))^2$$

$$SS_{res} = (11 - 9.78)^2 + (8.5 - 10.75)^2 + \cdots + (11 - 13.68)^2 \approx 19.20$$

Finally, we can find R-squared using the following:

$$R^2 = 1 - \frac{SS_{res}}{SS_{tot}}$$

$$R^2 = 1 - \frac{19.20}{56.8} \approx 0.66$$

The R-squared score of *0.662* indicates that a large proportion of the variance in the test instances' prices is explained by the model. Now let's confirm our calculation using scikit-learn. The `score` method of `LinearRegression` returns the model's R-squared value, as seen in the following example:

```
# In[1]:
import numpy as np
from sklearn.linear_model import LinearRegression

X_train = np.array([6, 8, 10, 14, 18]).reshape(-1, 1)
y_train = [7, 9, 13, 17.5, 18]

X_test = np.array([8, 9, 11, 16, 12]).reshape(-1, 1)
y_test = [11, 8.5, 15, 18, 11]

model = LinearRegression()
model.fit(X_train, y_train)
r_squared = model.score(X_test, y_test)
print(r_squared )

# Out[1]:
0.6620
```

Summary

In this chapter, we introduced simple linear regression, which models the relationship between a single explanatory variable and a continuous response variable. We worked through a toy problem to predict the price of a pizza from its diameter. We used the residual sum of squares cost function to assess the fitness of our model, and analytically solved the values of our model's parameter that minimized the cost function. We measured the performance of our model on a test set. Finally, we introduced scikit-learn's estimator API. In the next chapter, we will compare and contrast simple linear regression with another simple, ubiquitous model, **k-Nearest Neighbors (KNN)**.

3
Classification and Regression with k-Nearest Neighbors

In this chapter, we will introduce **k-Nearest Neighbors** (**KNN**), a simple algorithm that can be used for classification and regression tasks. KNN's simplicity belies its power and usefulness; it is widely used in the real world in a variety of applications, including search and recommender systems. We will compare and contrast KNN with simple linear regression and work through toy problems to understand the model.

K-Nearest Neighbors

KNN is a simple model for regression and classification tasks. It is so simple that its name describes most of its learning algorithm. The titular neighbors are representations of training instances in a **metric space**. A metric space is a feature space in which the distances between all members of a set are defined. In the previous chapter's pizza problem, our training instances were represented in a metric space because the distances between all the pizza diameters was defined. These neighbors are used to estimate the value of the response variable for a test instance. The hyperparameter k specifies how many neighbors can be used in the estimation. A hyperparameter is a parameter that controls how the algorithm learns; hyperparameters are not estimated from the training data and are sometimes set manually. Finally, the k neighbors that are selected are those that are nearest to the test instance, as measured by some distance function.

For classification tasks, a set of tuples of feature vectors and class labels comprise the training set. KNN is a capable of binary, multi-class, and multi-label classification; we will define these tasks later, and we will focus on binary classification in this chapter. The simplest KNN classifiers use the mode of the KNN labels to classify test instances, but other strategies can be used. The k is often set to an odd number to prevent ties. In regression tasks, the feature vectors are each associated with a response variable that takes a real-valued scalar instead of a label. The prediction is the mean or weighted mean of the KNN response variables.

Lazy learning and non-parametric models

KNN is a **lazy learner**. Also known as **instance-based learners**, lazy learners simply store the training dataset with little or no processing. In contrast to **eager learners** such as simple linear regression, KNN does not estimate the parameters of a model that generalizes the training data during a training phase. Lazy learning has advantages and disadvantages. Training an eager learner is often computationally costly, but prediction with the resulting model is often inexpensive. For simple linear regression, prediction consists only of multiplying the learned coefficient by the feature, and adding the learned intercept parameter. A lazy learner can predict almost immediately, but making predictions can be costly. In the simplest implementation of KNN, prediction requires calculating the distances between a test instance and all training instances.

In contrast to most of the other models that we will discuss, KNN is a **non-parametric model**. A **parametric model** uses a fixed number of parameters, or coefficients, to define the model that summarizes the data. The number of parameters is independent of the number of training instances. Non-parametric may seem to be a misnomer, as it does not mean that the model has no parameters; rather, non-parametric means that the number of parameters of the model is not fixed, and may grow with the number of training instances.

Non-parametric models can be useful when training data is abundant and you have little prior knowledge about the relationship between the response and explanatory variables. KNN makes only one assumption: instances that are near each other are likely to have similar values of the response variable. The flexibility provided by non-parametric models is not always desirable; a model that makes assumptions about the relationship can be useful if training data is scarce or if you already know about the relationship.

Classification with KNN

Recall from `Chapter 1`, *The Fundamentals of Machine Learning* that the goal of classification tasks is to use one or more features to predict the value of a discrete response variable. Let's work through a toy classification problem. Assume that you must use a person's height and weight to predict his or her sex. This problem is called **binary classification** because the response variable can take one of two labels. The following table records nine training instances:

Height	Weight	Label
158 cm	64 kg	male
170 cm	66 kg	male
183 cm	84 kg	male
191 cm	80 kg	male
155 cm	49 kg	female
163 cm	59 kg	female
180 cm	67 kg	female
158 cm	54 kg	female
178 cm	77 kg	female

Unlike the previous chapter's simple linear regression problem, we are now using features from two explanatory variables to predict the value of the response variable. KNN is not limited to two features; the algorithm can use an arbitrary number of features, but more than three features cannot be visualized. Let's visualize the data by creating a scatter plot with `matplotlib`:

```
# In[1]:
import numpy as np
import matplotlib.pyplot as plt

X_train = np.array([
  [158, 64],
  [170, 86],
  [183, 84],
  [191, 80],
  [155, 49],
  [163, 59],
  [180, 67],
```

```
  [158, 54],
  [170, 67]
])
y_train = ['male', 'male', 'male', 'male', 'female', 'female', 'female',
  'female', 'female']

plt.figure()
plt.title('Human Heights and Weights by Sex')
plt.xlabel('Height in cm')
plt.ylabel('Weight in kg')

for i, x in enumerate(X_train):
# Use 'x' markers for instances that are male and diamond markers for
instances that are female
plt.scatter(x[0], x[1], c='k', marker='x' if y_train[i] == 'male' else 'D')
plt.grid(True)
plt.show()
```

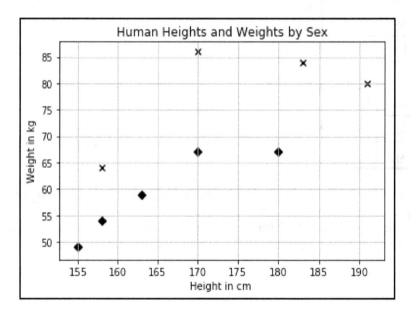

From the plot we can see that men, denoted by the **x** markers, tend to be taller and weigh more than women. This observation is probably consistent with your experience. Now let's use KNN to predict whether a person with a given height and weight is a man or a woman. Let's assume that we want to predict the sex of a person who is **155** cm tall and who weighs **70** kg. First, we must define our distance measure. In this case, we will use Euclidean distance, the straight line distance between points in a Euclidean space. Euclidean distance in a two-dimensional space is given by the following formula:

$$d(p,q) = d(q,p) = \sqrt{(q_1 - p_1)^2 + (q_2 - p_2)^2}$$

Next we must calculate the distances between the query instance and all the training instances:

Height	Weight	Label	Distance from test instance
158 cm	64 kg	male	$\sqrt{(158-155)^2 + (64-70)^2} = 6.71$
170 cm	66 kg	male	$\sqrt{(170-155)^2 + (64-70)^2} = 21.93$
183 cm	84 kg	male	$\sqrt{(183-155)^2 + (84-70)^2} = 31.30$
191 cm	80 kg	male	$\sqrt{(191-155)^2 + (80-70)^2} = 37.36$
155 cm	49 kg	female	$\sqrt{(155-155)^2 + (49-70)^2} = 21.00$
163 cm	59 kg	female	$\sqrt{(163-155)^2 + (59-70)^2} = 13.60$
180 cm	67 kg	female	$\sqrt{(180-155)^2 + (67-70)^2} = 25.18$
158 cm	54 kg	female	$\sqrt{(158-155)^2 + (54-70)^2} = 16.28$
178 cm	77 kg	female	$\sqrt{(178-155)^2 + (77-70)^2} = 24.04$

We will set k to 3 and select the three nearest training instances. The following script calculates the distances between the test instance and the training instances, and identifies the most common sex of the nearest neighbors:

```
# In[2]:
x = np.array([[155, 70]])
distances = np.sqrt(np.sum((X_train - x)**2, axis=1))
distances

# Out[2]:
array([ 6.70820393, 21.9317122 , 31.30495168, 37.36308338, 21. ,
13.60147051, 25.17935662, 16.2788206 , 15.29705854])

# In[3]:
nearest_neighbor_indices = distances.argsort()[:3]
nearest_neighbor_genders = np.take(y_train, nearest_neighbor_indices)
nearest_neighbor_genders

# Out[3]:
array(['male', 'female', 'female'], dtype='|S6')

# In[4]:
from collections import Counter
b = Counter(np.take(y_train, distances.argsort()[:3]))
b.most_common(1)[0][0]

# Out[4]:
'female'
```

The following plots the query instance, indicated by the circle, and its three nearest neighbors, indicated by the enlarged markers:

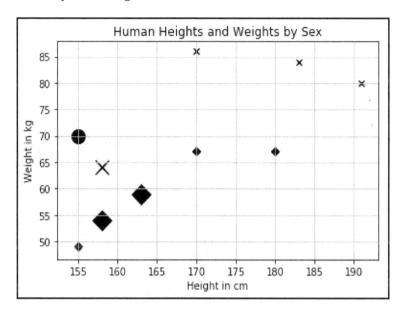

Two of the neighbors are female and one is male. We therefore predict that the test instance is female. Now let's implement a KNN classifier using scikit-learn:

```
# In[5]:
from sklearn.preprocessing import LabelBinarizer
from sklearn.neighbors import KNeighborsClassifier

lb = LabelBinarizer()
y_train_binarized = lb.fit_transform(y_train)
y_train_binarized

# Out[5]:
array([[1],
       [1],
       [1],
       [1],
       [0],
       [0],
       [0],
       [0],
       [0]])

# In[6]:
K = 3
```

```
clf = KNeighborsClassifier(n_neighbors=K)
clf.fit(X_train, y_train_binarized.reshape(-1))
prediction_binarized = clf.predict(np.array([155, 70]).reshape(1,
    -1))[0]
predicted_label = lb.inverse_transform(prediction_binarized)
predicted_label

# Out[6]:
array(['female'],
      dtype='|S6')
```

Our labels are strings; we first use LabelBinarizer to convert them to integers. LabelBinarizer implements the **transformer interface**, which consists of the methods fit, transform, and fit_transform. The fit method prepares the transformer; in this case, it creates a mapping from label strings to integers. The transform method applies the mapping to input labels. The fit_transform method is a convenience method that calls fit and transform. A transformer should be fit only on the training set. Independently fitting and transforming the training and testing sets could result in inconsistent mappings from labels to integers; in this case, male might be mapped to 1 in the training set and 0 in the testing set. Fitting on the entire dataset should also be avoided because for some transformers it will leak information about the testing set into the model. This advantage won't be available in production, so performance measures on the test set may be optimistic. We will discuss this pitfall more when we extract features from text.

Next, we initialize KNeighborsClassifier. Even though KNN is a lazy learner, it still implements the estimator interface. We call fit and predict just as we did with our simple linear regression object. Finally, we can use our fit LabelBinarizer to reverse the transformation and return a string label. Now let's use our classifier to make predictions for a test set, and evaluate the performance of our classifier:

Height	Weight	Label
168 cm	65 kg	male
170 cm	61 kg	male
160 cm	52 kg	female
169 cm	67 kg	female

```
# In[7]:
X_test = np.array([
  [168, 65],
  [180, 96],
  [160, 52],
  [169, 67]
```

```
])
y_test = ['male', 'male', 'female', 'female']
y_test_binarized = lb.transform(y_test)
print('Binarized labels: %s' % y_test_binarized.T[0])
predictions_binarized = clf.predict(X_test)
print('Binarized predictions: %s' % predictions_binarized)
print('Predicted labels: %s' % lb.inverse_transform(predictions_binarized))

# Out[7]:
Binarized labels: [1 1 0 0]
Binarized predictions: [0 1 0 0]
Predicted labels: ['female' 'male' 'female' 'female']
```

By comparing our test labels to our classifier's predictions, we find that it incorrectly predicted that one of the `male` test instances was `female`. Recall from Chapter 1, *The Fundamentals of Machine Learning,* that there are two types of errors in binary classification tasks: false positives and false negatives. There are many performance measures for classifiers; some measures may be more appropriate than others depending on the consequences of the types of errors in your application. We will assess our classifier using several common performance measures, including accuracy, precision, and recall. Accuracy is the proportion of test instances that were classified correctly. Our model classified one of the four instances incorrectly, so the accuracy is *75%*:

```
# In[8]:
from sklearn.metrics import accuracy_score
print('Accuracy: %s' % accuracy_score(y_test_binarized,
    predictions_binarized))

# Out[8]:
Accuracy: 0.75
```

Precision is the proportion of test instances that were predicted to be positive that are truly positive. In this example, the positive class is `male`. The assignment of `male` and `female` to the positive and negative classes is arbitrary, and could be reversed. Our classifier predicted that one of the test instances is the positive class. This instance is truly the positive class, so the classifier's precision is *100%*:

```
# In[9]:
from sklearn.metrics import precision_score
print('Precision: %s' % precision_score(y_test_binarized,
  predictions_binarized))

# Out[9]:
Precision: 1.0
```

Recall is the proportion of truly positive test instances that were predicted to be positive. Our classifier predicted that one of the two truly positive test instances is positive. Its recall is therefore *50%*:

```
# In[10]:
from sklearn.metrics import recall_score
print('Recall: %s' % recall_score(y_test_binarized,
    predictions_binarized))

# Out[10]:
Recall: 0.5
```

Sometimes it is useful to summarize precision and recall with a single statistic, called the **F1 score** or **F1 measure**. The F1 score is the harmonic mean of precision and recall:

```
# In[11]:
from sklearn.metrics import f1_score
print('F1 score: %s' % f1_score(y_test_binarized,
    predictions_binarized))

# Out[11]:
F1 score: 0.666666666667
```

Note that the arithmetic mean of the precision and recall scores is the upper bound of the F1 score. The F1 score penalizes classifiers more as the difference between their precision and recall scores increases. Finally, the **Matthews correlation coefficient** (MCC)is an alternative to the F1 score for measuring the performance of binary classifiers. A perfect classifier's MCC is *1*. A trivial classifier that predicts randomly will score *0*, and a perfectly wrong classifier will score *-1*. MCC is useful even when the proportions of the classes in the test set is severely imbalanced:

```
# In[12]:
from sklearn.metrics import matthews_corrcoef
print('Matthews correlation coefficient: %s' %
matthews_corrcoef(y_test_binarized, predictions_binarized))

# Out[12]:
Matthews correlation coefficient: 0.57735026919
```

scikit-learn also provides a convenience function, `classification_report`, that reports the precision, recall, and F1 score:

```
# In[13]:
from sklearn.metrics import classification_report
print(classification_report(y_test_binarized, predictions_binarized,
target_names=['male'], labels=[1]))
```

```
# Out[13]:
            precision  recall  f1-score  support
    male         1.00    0.50      0.67        2
avg / total      1.00    0.50      0.67        2
```

Regression with KNN

Now let's use KNN for a regression task. Let's use a person's height and sex to predict their weight. The following tables list our training and testing sets:

Height	Sex	Weight
158 cm	male	64 kg
170 cm	male	66 kg
183 cm	male	84 kg
191 cm	male	80 kg
155 cm	female	49 kg
163 cm	female	59 kg
180 cm	female	67 kg
158 cm	fcmale	54 kg
178 cm	female	77 kg

Height	Sex	Weight
168 cm	male	65 kg
170 cm	male	61 kg
160 cm	female	52 kg
169 cm	female	67 kg

We will instantiate and fit `KNeighborsRegressor`, and use it to predict weights. In this dataset, sex has already been coded as a binary-valued feature. Notice that this feature ranges from *0* to *1*, while the values of the feature representing the person's height range from *155* to *191*. We will discuss why this is a problem, and how it can be ameliorated, in the next section. In the pizza price problem, we used the coefficient of determination to measure the performance of our model. We will use it to measure the performance of our regressor again, and introduce two more performance measures for regression tasks--**Mean Absolute Error (MAE)** and **Mean Squared Error (MSE)**:

```
# In[1]:
import numpy as np
from sklearn.neighbors import KNeighborsRegressor
from sklearn.metrics import mean_absolute_error, mean_squared_error,
  r2_score

X_train = np.array([
  [158, 1],
  [170, 1],
  [183, 1],
  [191, 1],
  [155, 0],
  [163, 0],
  [180, 0],
  [158, 0],
  [170, 0]
])
y_train = [64, 86, 84, 80, 49, 59, 67, 54, 67]

X_test = np.array([
  [168, 1],
  [180, 1],
  [160, 0],
  [169, 0]
])
y_test = [65, 96, 52, 67]

K = 3
clf = KNeighborsRegressor(n_neighbors=K)
clf.fit(X_train, y_train)
predictions = clf.predict(X_test)
print('Predicted wieghts: %s' % predictions)
print('Coefficient of determination: %s' % r2_score(y_test,
  predictions))
print('Mean absolute error: %s' % mean_absolute_error(y_test,
  predictions))
print('Mean squared error: %s' % mean_squared_error(y_test,
  predictions))
```

```
# Out[1]:
Predicted wieghts: [ 70.66666667  79.           59.           70.66666667]
Coefficient of determination: 0.629056522674
Mean absolute error: 8.33333333333
Mean squared error: 95.8888888889
```

MAE is the average of the absolute values of the errors of the predictions. *MAE* is given by the following:

$$MAE = \frac{1}{n} \sum_{i=0}^{n-1} |y_i - \hat{y}_i|$$

MSE, or **Mean Squared Deviation (MSD)**, is a more common alternative to mean absolute error. Given by the following equation, *MSE* is the average of the squares of the errors of the predictions:

$$MSE = \frac{1}{n} \sum_{i=0}^{n-1} (y_i - \hat{y}_i)^2$$

It is important that regression performance measures disregard the directions of the errors; otherwise, the errors of a regressor that under- and over-predicts equally would cancel out. MSE and MAE accomplish this by squaring errors and taking the absolute values of errors, respectively. MSE penalizes outliers more than MAE; squaring a large error makes it contribute disproportionately more to the total error. This may be desirable in some problems, but MSE is often preferred even when it is not, as MSE has useful mathematical properties. Note that ordinary linear regression, such as the previous chapter's simple linear regression problem, minimizes the square root of the MSE.

Scaling features

Many learning algorithms work better when features take similar ranges of values. In the previous section, we used two features: a binary-valued feature representing the person's sex and a continuous-valued feature representing the person's height in centimeters. Consider a dataset in which we have a man who is *170* cm tall and a woman who is *160* cm tall.

Which instance is closer to a man who is *164* cm tall? For our weight prediction problem, we probably believe that the query is closer to the male instance; a *6* cm difference in height is less important to predicting weight than the difference between sexes. If we represent the height in millimeters, the query instance is closer to the *1600* mm tall female. If we represent the height in meters, the query instance is closer to the *1.7* meter tall male. If we represent the heights in micrometers, the height feature would dominate the distance function even more:

```
# In[2]:
from scipy.spatial.distance import euclidean

# heights in millimeters
X_train = np.array([
  [1700, 1],
  [1600, 0]
])
x_test = np.array([1640, 1]).reshape(1, -1)
print(euclidean(X_train[0, :], x_test))
print(euclidean(X_train[1, :], x_test))

# heights in meters
X_train = np.array([
  [1.7, 1],
  [1.6, 0]
])
x_test = np.array([164, 1]).reshape(1, -1)
print(euclidean(X_train[0, :], x_test))
print(euclidean(X_train[1, :], x_test))

# Out[2]:
8.0
2.2360679775
160.3
160.4031171766933
```

scikit-learn's `StandardScaler` is a transformer that scales features so that they have unit variance. It first centers features by subtracting the mean of each feature from each instance's value of the feature. It then scales the features by dividing each instance's value of the feature by the standard deviation of the feature. Data that has zero mean and unit variance is **standardized**. Like `LabelBinarizer`, `StandardScaler` implements the transformer interface. Let's standardize the previous problem's features, fit the regressor again, and compare the performances of the two models:

```
# In[3]:
from sklearn.preprocessing import StandardScaler
ss = StandardScaler()
```

```
X_train_scaled = ss.fit_transform(X_train)

print(X_train)
print(X_train_scaled)

X_test_scaled = ss.transform(X_test)

clf.fit(X_train_scaled, y_train)
predictions = clf.predict(X_test_scaled)
print('Predicted wieghts: %s' % predictions)
print('Coefficient of determination: %s' % r2_score(y_test,
    predictions))
print('Mean absolute error: %s' % mean_absolute_error(y_test,
    predictions))
print('Mean squared error: %s' % mean_squared_error(y_test,
    predictions))

# Out[3]:
[[158    1]
 [170    1]
 [183    1]
 [191    1]
 [155    0]
 [163    0]
 [180    0]
 [158    0]
 [170    0]]
[[-0.9908706   1.11803399]
 [ 0.01869567  1.11803399]
 [ 1.11239246  1.11803399]
 [ 1.78543664  1.11803399]
 [-1.24326216 -0.89442719]
 [-0.57021798 -0.89442719]
 [ 0.86000089 -0.89442719]
 [-0.9908706  -0.89442719]
 [ 0.01869567 -0.89442719]]
Predicted wieghts: [ 78.          83.33333333  54.          64.33333333]
Coefficient of determination: 0.670642596175
Mean absolute error: 7.58333333333
Mean squared error: 85.1388888889
```

Our model performs better on standardized data. The feature representing the person's sex contributes more to the distance between instances and allows the model to make better predictions.

Summary

In this chapter, we introduced KNN, a simple but powerful model that can be used in classification and regression tasks. KNN is a lazy learner and a non-parametric model; it does not estimate the values of a fixed number of parameters from the training data. Instead, it stores all the training instances and uses the instances that are nearest the test instance to predict the value of the response variable. We worked through toy classification and regression problems. We also introduced scikit-learn's transformer interface; we used `LabelBinarizer` to transform string labels to binary labels and `StandardScaler` to standardize our features.

In the next chapter, we will discuss feature extraction techniques for categorical variables, text, and images; these will allow us to apply KNN to more problems in the real world.

4

Feature Extraction

The examples discussed in the previous chapters used real-valued explanatory variables, such as the diameter of a pizza. Many machine learning problems require learning from categorical variables, text, or images. In this chapter, we will learn to create features that represent such variables.

Extracting features from categorical variables

Many problems have explanatory variables that are **categorical** or **nominal**. A categorical variable can take one of a fixed set of values. For example, an application that predicts the salary for a job might use categorical variables such as the city in which the position is located. Categorical variables are commonly encoded using **one-of-k encoding**, or **one-hot encoding**, in which the explanatory variable is represented using one binary feature for each of its possible values.

For example, let's assume our model has a `city` variable that can take one of three values: `New York`, `San Francisco`, or `Chapel Hill`. One-hot encoding represents the variable using one binary feature for each of the three possible cities. scikit-learn's `DictVectorizer` class is a transformer that can be used to one-hot encode categorical features:

```
# In[1]:
from sklearn.feature_extraction import DictVectorizer
onehot_encoder = DictVectorizer()
X = [
    {'city': 'New York'},
    {'city': 'San Francisco'},
    {'city': 'Chapel Hill'}
]
```

```
print(onehot_encoder.fit_transform(X).toarray())

# Out[1]:
[[ 0.   1.   0.]
 [ 0.   0.   1.]
 [ 1.   0.   0.]]
```

Note that the order of the features in the resulting vectors is arbitrary. In the first training example, the value of `city` is `New York`. The second element in the feature vector corresponds to the `New York` value, and it is equal to one for the first instance.

It may seem intuitive to represent the values of a categorical explanatory variable with a single integer feature. `New York` could be represented by zero, `San Francisco` by one, and `Chapel Hill` by two, for example. The problem is that this representation encodes artificial information. Representing cities with integers encodes an order for cities that does not exist in the real world, and facilitates comparisons of them that do not make sense. There is no natural order of cities by which `Chapel Hill` is one more than `San Francisco`. One-hot encoding avoids this problem and only represents the value of the variable.

Standardizing features

We learned in the previous chapter that many learning algorithms perform better when they are trained on standardized data. Recall that standardized data has zero mean and unit variance. An explanatory variable with zero mean is centered about the origin; its average value is zero. A feature vector has unit variance when the variances of its features are all of the same order of magnitude. If one feature's variance is orders of magnitude greater than the variances of the other features, that feature may dominate the learning algorithm and prevent it from learning from the other variables. Some learning algorithms also converge to the optimal parameter values more slowly when data is not standardized. In addition to the `StandardScaler` transformer we used in the previous chapter, the `scale` function from the `preprocessing` module can be used to standardize a dataset along any axis:

```
# In[1]:
from sklearn import preprocessing
import numpy as np
X = np.array([
  [0., 0., 5., 13., 9., 1.],
  [0., 0., 13., 15., 10., 15.],
  [0., 3., 15., 2., 0., 11.]
])
print(preprocessing.scale(X))
```

```
# Out[1]:
[[ 0.          -0.70710678 -1.38873015  0.52489066  0.59299945
   -1.35873244]
 [ 0.          -0.70710678  0.46291005  0.87481777  0.81537425
   1.01904933]
 [ 0.           1.41421356  0.9258201  -1.39970842 -1.4083737
   0.33968311]]
```

Finally, `RobustScaler` is an alternative to `StandardScaler` that is robust to outliers. `StandardScaler` subtracts the mean of a feature from each instance's value, and divides by the feature's standard deviation. To mitigate the effect of large outliers, `RobustScaler` subtracts the median and divides by the **interquartile range**. Quartiles are calculated by splitting the sorted dataset into four parts of equal size. The median is the second quartile; the interquartile range is the difference of the third and first quartiles.

Extracting features from text

Many machine learning problems use text, which usually represents natural language. Text must be transformed to a vector representation that encodes some aspect of its meaning. In the following sections, we will review variations of two of the most common representation of text that are used in machine learning: the bag-of-words model and word embeddings.

The bag-of-words model

The most common representation of text is the **bag-of-words model**. This representation uses a multiset, or bag, that encodes the words that appear in a text; bag-of-words does not encode any of the text's syntax, ignores the order of words, and disregards all grammar. Bag-of-words can be thought of as an extension to one-hot encoding. It creates one feature for each word of interest in the text. The bag-of-words model is motivated by the intuition that documents containing similar words often have similar meanings. The bag-of-words model can be used effectively for document classification and retrieval despite the limited information that it encodes. A collection of documents is called a **corpus**. Let's use a corpus with the following two documents to examine the bag-of-words model:

```
# In[1]:
corpus = [
    'UNC played Duke in basketball',
    'Duke lost the basketball game'
]
```

This corpus contains eight unique words. The corpus's unique words comprise its vocabulary. The bag-of-words model uses a feature vector with an element for each of the words in the corpus's vocabulary to represent each document. Our corpus has eight unique words, so each document will be represented by a vector with eight elements. The number of elements that comprise a feature vector is called the **vector's dimension**. A dictionary maps the vocabulary to indices in the feature vector.

> The dictionary for a bag-of-words could be implemented using a Python `Dictionary`, but the Python data structure and the representation's mapping are distinct.

In the most basic bag-of-words representation, each element in the feature vector is a binary value that represents whether or not the corresponding word appeared in the document. For example, the first word in the first document is UNC. UNC is the first word in the dictionary, so the first element in the vector is equal to one. The last word in the dictionary is game. The first document does not contain the word game, so the eighth element in its vector is set to zero. The `CountVectorizer` transformer can produce a bag-of-words representation from a string or file. By default, `CountVectorizer` converts the characters in the documents to lowercase and **tokenizes** the documents. Tokenization is the process of splitting a string into tokens, or meaningful sequences of characters. Tokens are often words, but they may also be shorter sequences, including punctuation characters and affixes. `CountVectorizer` tokenizes using a regular expression that splits strings on whitespace and extracts sequences of characters that are two or more characters in length. The documents in our corpus are represented by the following feature vectors:

```
# In[2]:
from sklearn.feature_extraction.text import CountVectorizer
vectorizer = CountVectorizer()
print(vectorizer.fit_transform(corpus).todense())
print(vectorizer.vocabulary_)

# Out[2]:
[[1 1 0 1 0 1 0 1]
 [1 1 1 0 1 0 1 0]]
{'played': 5, 'the': 6, 'in': 3, 'lost': 4, 'game': 2, 'basketball': 0,
    'unc': 7,'duke': 1}
```

Our corpus's dictionary now contains the following ten unique words. Note that I and a were not extracted as they do not match the regular expression. Now let's add a third document to our corpus and inspect the dictionary and feature vectors:

```
# In[3]:
corpus.append('I ate a sandwich')
print(vectorizer.fit_transform(corpus).todense())
print(vectorizer.vocabulary_)

# Out[3]:
[[0 1 1 0 1 0 1 0 0 1]
 [0 1 1 1 0 1 0 0 1 0]
 [1 0 0 0 0 0 0 1 0 0]]
{'played': 6, 'the': 8, 'in': 4, 'game': 3, 'lost': 5, 'ate': 0,
  'sandwich': 7,'basketball': 1, 'unc': 9, 'duke': 2}
```

The meanings of the first two documents are more similar to each other than they are to the third document, and their corresponding feature vectors are more similar to each other than they are to the third document's feature vector when using a metric such as **Euclidean distance**. The Euclidean distance between two vectors is equal to the **Euclidean norm**, or **L^2 norm**, of the difference between the two vectors, as given by this equation:

$$d = \|x_0 - x_1\|$$

A **norm** is a function that assigns a positive size to a vector. The Euclidean norm of a vector is equal to the vector's **magnitude**, which is given by the following equation:

$$\|x\| = \sqrt{x_1^2 + x_2^2 + \ldots + x_n^2}$$

scikit-learn's `euclidean_distances` function can be used to calculate the distance between two or more vectors, and confirms that the most semantically similar documents are also the closest to each other in the vector space. In the following example, we will use the `euclidean_distances` function to compare the feature vectors for our documents:

```
# In[4]:
from sklearn.metrics.pairwise import euclidean_distances
X = vectorizer.fit_transform(corpus).todense()
print('Distance between 1st and 2nd documents:',
   euclidean_distances(X[0], X[1]))
print('Distance between 1st and 3rd documents:',
    euclidean_distances(X[0], X[2]))
print('Distance between 2nd and 3rd documents:',
```

```
    euclidean_distances(X[1], X[2]))

# Out[4]:
Distance between 1st and 2nd documents: [[ 2.44948974]]
Distance between 1st and 3rd documents: [[ 2.64575131]]
Distance between 2nd and 3rd documents: [[ 2.64575131]]
```

Now let's assume that we are using a corpus of news articles instead of our toy corpus. Our dictionary may now have hundreds of thousands of unique words instead of only *12*. The feature vectors representing the articles will each have hundreds of thousands of elements, and many of the elements will be zero. Most sports articles will not have any of the words particular to finance articles, and most culture articles will not have any of the words particular to articles about politics. High-dimensional vectors that have many zero-valued elements are called **sparse vectors**.

Using high-dimensional data creates several problems for all machine learning tasks, including those that do not involve text. Collectively, these problems are known as the **curse of dimensionality**. The first problem is that high-dimensional vectors require more memory and computation than low-dimensional vectors. SciPy provides some data types that mitigate this problem by efficiently representing only the non-zero elements of sparse vectors. The second problem is that as the feature space's dimensionality increases, more training data is required to ensure that there are enough training instances with each combination of the feature's values. If there are insufficient training instances for a feature, the algorithm may overfit noise in the training data and fail to generalize. In the following sections, we will review several strategies for reducing the dimensionality of text features. In later chapters, we will review more techniques for dimensionality reduction.

Stop word filtering

A basic strategy for reducing the dimensions of the feature space is to convert all of the text to lowercase. This is motivated by the insight that the letter case does not contribute to the meanings of most words; *sandwich* and *Sandwich* have the same meaning in most contexts. Capitalization may indicate that a word is beginning a sentence, but the bag-of-words model has already discarded all information from word order and grammar.

A second strategy is to remove words that are common to most of the documents in the corpus. These words, called **stop words**, frequently include determiners such as "the", "a", and "an"; auxiliary verbs such as "do", "be", and "will"; and prepositions such as "on", "around", and "beneath". Stop words are often functional words that contribute to the document's meaning through grammar rather than their denotations. `CountVectorizer` can filter stop words provided as the `stop_words` keyword parameter, and also includes a basic list of English stop words.

Let's re-create the feature vectors for our documents using stop word filtering:

```
# In[5]:
vectorizer = CountVectorizer(stop_words='english')
print(vectorizer.fit_transform(corpus).todense())
print(vectorizer.vocabulary_)

# Out[5]:
[[0 1 1 0 0 1 0 1]
 [0 1 1 1 1 0 0 0]
 [1 0 0 0 0 0 1 0]]
{'played': 5, 'game': 3, 'lost': 4, 'ate': 0, 'sandwich': 6,
    'basketball': 1,'unc': 7, 'duke': 2}
```

The feature vectors now have fewer dimensions, and the first two document vectors are still more similar to each other than they are to the third document.

Stemming and lemmatization

While stop word filtering is an easy strategy for dimensionality reduction, most stop word lists contain only a few hundred words. A large corpus may still have hundreds of thousands of unique words after filtering. Two similar strategies for further reducing dimensionality are called **stemming** and **lemmatization**.

A high-dimensional document vector may separately encode several derived or inflected forms of the same word. For example, "jumping" and "jumps" are both forms of the word "jump"; a document vector in a corpus of long-jumping articles may encode each inflected form with a separate element in the feature vector. Stemming and lemmatization are two strategies for condensing inflected and derived forms of a word into a single feature. Let's consider another toy corpus with two documents:

```
# In[6]:
corpus = [
    'He ate the sandwiches',
    'Every sandwich was eaten by him'
]
vectorizer = CountVectorizer(binary=True, stop_words='english')
print(vectorizer.fit_transform(corpus).todense())
print(vectorizer.vocabulary_)

# Out[6]:
[[1 0 0 1]
 [0 1 1 0]]
{'ate': 0, 'eaten': 1, 'sandwich': 2, 'sandwiches': 3}
```

The documents have similar meanings, but their feature vectors have no elements in common! Both documents contain a conjugation of `ate` and a form of `sandwich`. Ideally, these similarities should be reflected in the feature vectors. Lemmatization is the process of determining the lemma, or the morphological root, of an inflected word based on its context. Lemmas are the base forms of words that are used to key the word in a dictionary. Stemming has a similar goal to lemmatization, but it does not attempt to produce the morphological roots of words. Instead, stemming removes all patterns of characters that appear to be affixes, resulting in a token that is not necessarily a valid word. Lemmatization frequently requires a lexical resource, like WordNet, and the word's part-of-speech. Stemming algorithms frequently use rules instead of lexical resources to produce stems and can operate on any token, even without its context. Let's consider lemmatization of the word `gathering` in two documents:

```
# In[7]:
corpus = [
    'I am gathering ingredients for the sandwich.',
    'There were many wizards at the gathering.'
]
```

In the first sentence, `gathering` is a verb, and its lemma is `gather`. In the second sentence, `gathering` is a noun, and its lemma is `gathering`. We will use the **Natural Language Tool Kit (NLTK)** to stem and lemmatize the corpus. NLTK can be installed by following the instructions at `http://www.nltk.org/install.html`. Using the parts of speech of `gathering`, NLTK's `WordNetLemmatizer` correctly lemmatizes the words in both documents:

```
# In[8]:
from nltk.stem.wordnet import WordNetLemmatizer
lemmatizer = WordNetLemmatizer()
print(lemmatizer.lemmatize('gathering', 'v'))
print(lemmatizer.lemmatize('gathering', 'n'))

# Out[8]:
gather
gathering
```

Let's compare lemmatization with stemming. `PorterStemmer` cannot consider the inflected form's part-of-speech and returns `gather` for both documents:

```
# In[9]:
from nltk.stem import PorterStemmer
stemmer = PorterStemmer()
print(stemmer.stem('gathering'))

# Out[9]:
gather
```

Now let's lemmatize our toy corpus:

```
# In[1]:
from nltk import word_tokenize
from nltk.stem import PorterStemmer
from nltk.stem.wordnet import WordNetLemmatizer
from nltk import pos_tag

wordnet_tags = ['n', 'v']
corpus = [
    'He ate the sandwiches',
    'Every sandwich was eaten by him'
]
stemmer = PorterStemmer()
print('Stemmed:', [[stemmer.stem(token) for token in
word_tokenize(document)] for document in corpus])


def lemmatize(token, tag):
    if tag[0].lower() in ['n', 'v']:
        return lemmatizer.lemmatize(token, tag[0].lower())
    return token

lemmatizer = WordNetLemmatizer()
tagged_corpus = [pos_tag(word_tokenize(document)) for document in
  corpus]
print('Lemmatized:', [[lemmatize(token, tag) for token, tag in
  document] for document in tagged_corpus])

# Out[1]:
Stemmed: [['He', 'ate', 'the', 'sandwich'], ['everi', 'sandwich', 'wa',
  'eaten', 'by', 'him']]
Lemmatized: [['He', 'eat', 'the', 'sandwich'], ['Every', 'sandwich',
  'be', 'eat', 'by', 'him']]
```

Through stemming and lemmatization, we reduced the dimensionality of our feature space. We produced feature representations that more effectively encode the meanings of the documents despite the fact that the words in the corpus's dictionary are inflected differently in the sentences.

Extending bag-of-words with tf-idf weights

In the previous section, we used the bag-of-words representation to create feature vectors that encode whether or not a word from the corpus's dictionary appears in a document. These feature vectors do not encode grammar, word order, or the frequencies of words. It is intuitive that the frequency with which a word appears in a document could indicate the extent to which a document pertains to that word. A long document that contains one occurrence of a word may discuss an entirely different topic than a document that contains many occurrences of the same word. In this section, we will create feature vectors that encode the frequencies of words, and discuss strategies for mitigating two problems caused by encoding term frequencies. Instead of using a binary value for each element in the feature vector, we will now use an integer that represents the number of times that the words appeared in the document. With stop word filtering, the corpus is represented by the following feature vector:

```
# In[1]:
import numpy as np
from sklearn.feature_extraction.text import CountVectorizer

corpus = ['The dog ate a sandwich, the wizard transfigured a sandwich,
    and I ate a sandwich']
vectorizer = CountVectorizer(stop_words='english')
frequencies = np.array(vectorizer.fit_transform(corpus).todense())[0]
print(frequencies)
print('Token indices %s' % vectorizer.vocabulary_)
for token, index in vectorizer.vocabulary_.items():
    print('The token "%s" appears %s times' % (token,
        frequencies[index]))

# Out[1]:
[2 1 3 1 1]
Token indices {'ate': 0, 'sandwich': 2, 'dog': 1, 'wizard': 4,
    'transfigured': 3}
The token "ate" appears 2 times
The token "sandwich" appears 3 times
The token "dog" appears 1 times
The token "wizard" appears 1 times
The token "transfigured" appears 1 times
```

The element for dog (at index 1) is now set to one, and the element for sandwich (at index 2) is set to three to indicate that the corresponding words occurred one and three times, respectively. Note that the CountVectorizer binary parameter is omitted; its default value is False, which causes it to return raw term frequencies rather than binary frequencies. Encoding the terms' raw frequencies in the feature vector provides additional information about the meanings of the documents, but assumes that all the documents are of similar lengths. Many words might appear with the same frequency in two documents, but the documents could still be dissimilar if one document is many times larger than the other. scikit-learn's TfdfTransformer can mitigate this problem by transforming a matrix of term frequency vectors into a matrix of normalized term frequency weights. By default, TfdfTransformer smooths the raw counts and applies L^2 normalization. The smoothed, normalized term frequencies are given by this equation:

$$tf(t,d) = \frac{f(t,d)}{\|x\|}$$

The numerator is the frequency of the term in the document. The denominator is the L^2 norm of the term count vector. In addition to normalizing raw term counts, we can improve our feature vectors by calculating logarithmically scaled term frequencies, which scale the counts to a more limited range. Logarithmically scaled term frequencies are given by the following equation:

$$tf(t,d) = 1 + \log f(t,d)$$

TfdfTransformer calculates logarithmically scaled term frequencies when its sublinear_tf keyword parameter is set to True. Normalization and logarithmically scaled term frequencies can represent the frequencies of terms in a document while mitigating the effects of different document sizes. However, another problem remains with these representations. The feature vectors contain large weights for terms that occur frequently in a document, even if those terms occur frequently in most documents in the corpus. These terms do not help to represent the meaning of a particular document relative to the rest of the corpus. For example, most of the documents in a corpus of articles about Duke's basketball team could include the words Coach K, trip, and flop. These words can be thought of as corpus-specific stop words, and may not be useful for calculating the similarity of documents. The **Inverse Document Frequency (IDF)** is a measure of how rare or common a word is in a corpus.

The inverse document frequency is given by this equation:

$$idf\left(t,D\right) = \log\frac{N}{1+\left|d \in D : t \in d\right|}$$

Here, the numerator is the total number of documents in the corpus and the denominator is the number of documents in the corpus that contain the term. A term's tf-idf value is the product of its term frequency and inverse document frequency. `TfidfTransformer` returns tf-idf weights when its `use_idf` keyword argument is set to its default value, `True`. Since tf-idf weighted feature vectors are commonly used to represent text; scikit-learn provides a `TfidfVectorizer` transformer class that wraps `CountVectorizer` and `TfidfTransformer`. Let's use `TfidfVectorizer` to create tf-idf weighted feature vectors for our corpus:

```
# In[1]:
from sklearn.feature_extraction.text import TfidfVectorizer

corpus = [
    'The dog ate a sandwich and I ate a sandwich',
    'The wizard transfigured a sandwich'
]
vectorizer = TfidfVectorizer(stop_words='english')
print(vectorizer.fit_transform(corpus).todense())

# Out[1]:
[[ 0.75458397  0.37729199  0.53689271  0.         0.         ]
 [ 0.          0.          0.44943642  0.6316672  0.6316672 ]]
```

By comparing the tf-idf weights to the raw term frequencies, we can see that words that are common to many of the documents in the corpus, such as `sandwich`, have been penalized.

Space-efficient feature vectorizing with the hashing trick

In this chapter's previous examples, a dictionary containing all of the corpus's unique tokens is used to map a document's tokens to the elements of a feature vector. Creating this dictionary, however, has two drawbacks. First, two passes are required over the corpus: the first pass is used to create the dictionary, and the second pass is used to create feature vectors for the documents.

Second, the dictionary must be stored in memory, which could be prohibitively expensive for large corpora. It is possible to avoid creating this dictionary by applying a hash function to the token to determine its index in the feature vector directly. This shortcut is called the **hashing trick**:

```
# In[1]:
from sklearn.feature_extraction.text import HashingVectorizer

corpus = ['the', 'ate', 'bacon', 'cat']
vectorizer = HashingVectorizer(n_features=6)
print(vectorizer.transform(corpus).todense())

# Out[1]:
[[-1.  0.  0.  0.  0.  0.]
 [ 0.  0.  0.  1.  0.  0.]
 [ 0.  0.  0.  0. -1.  0.]
 [ 0.  1.  0.  0.  0.  0.]]
```

The hashing trick is stateless. Because the hashing trick does not require an initial pass over the corpus, it can be used to create feature vectors in both parallel and online, or streaming, applications. Note that n_features is an optional keyword argument. Its default value, 2^{20}, is adequate for most problems; it is set to six here so that the entire matrix will be small enough to print. Also note that some of the term frequencies are negative. Since hash collisions are possible, HashingVectorizer uses a signed hash function. The value of a feature takes the same sign as its token's hash; if the term cats appears twice in a document and is hashed to index negative three, the fourth element of the document's feature vector will be decremented by two (one for each occurrence of cat). If the term dogs also appears twice and is hashed to positive three, the fourth element of the feature vector will be incremented by two. Using a signed hash function creates the possibility that errors from hash collisions will cancel each other out rather than accumulate; but just a loss of information is preferable over a loss of information and addition of spurious information. Another disadvantage of the hashing trick is that the resulting model is more difficult to inspect, as the dictionary is not stored.

Word embeddings

Word embeddings are representations of text that mitigate some of the shortcomings of the bag-of-words model. While the bag-of-words model uses a scalar to represent each token, word embeddings use a vector. The vectors are usually dense and often have between *50* and *500* dimensions. These vectors represent the words in a metric space. Words that are semantically similar to each other are represented by vectors that are near each other. Concretely, word embeddings are parameterized functions that take a token from some language as an input and output a vector. This function is essentially a lookup table that is parameterized by a matrix of embeddings. How is this matrix learned?

The parameters of a word embedding function are typically learned through training a model for a different task. For example, let's consider training a language model that predicts whether a sequence of five words is probable in a some language. We will describe the model and learning algorithm in limited detail as we are only interested in how the word embedding parameters are produced.

Our dataset for this task consists of tuples of word sequences and binary labels that indicate whether or not the sequence is valid. Positive instances can be produced by extracting sequences of words from a large corpus, such as Google News, Wikipedia, or Common Crawl. Negative instances can be produced from positive instances by replacing a word in the sequence with a random word from the corpus; the resulting sequence will likely be nonsense. An example of a positive instance's sequence is `the Duke basketball player flopped`. An example of a negative instance is `the Duke basketball player potato`.

Our language model has two components. The first component is essentially our word embedding function; given a token, it outputs a vector. The second component is a binary classifier that predicts whether the five vectors represent a valid sequence of tokens. The parameters of the first component are initialized randomly, and updated as the classifier is trained. Replacing a word in a valid sequence with a word that has a similar meaning will likely result in a valid sequence. If the "the small cat is grumpy" and "the small kitten is grumpy" are both valid sequences, the model may represent "cat" and "kitten" using similar vectors. Replacing a word in a valid sequence with an unrelated word will likely result in an invalid sequence, and require the learning algorithm to update the parameters of the embedding function. The sequences *the* "small cat was grumpy" and "the small sandwich was grumpy" have all but one word in common; if the classifier is to learn that the latter is invalid, the vectors representing "cat" and "sandwich" must be dissimilar. Through learning to classify valid sequences of tokens, the model creates an embedding function that produces similar vectors for words with similar meanings. The vectors representing synonyms, such as "small" and "tiny", and coordinate terms, such as "UNC" and "Duke", should be similar. The vectors representing antonyms, such as "big" and "small", should be similar in all but one or a few dimensions.

Similarly, the vectors representing hypernyms and their hyponyms, such as "color" and "blue" or "furniture" and "chair", should differ in only a few dimensions.

Consider a corpus that contains the document *the* "dog was happy". Assume also that this corpus's vocabulary does not contain the tokens "puppy" or "sad". A sentiment analysis model trained on a bag-of-words representation of this corpus will be powerless when it encounters a sentence like "the dog was sad". A model trained on word embeddings will be able to generalize more effectively.

Let's inspect some word embeddings. Training a model like our example sequence classifier on a large corpus can be computationally costly, but the resulting word embeddings can be applied in many domains. For these reasons, it is common to use pre-trained word embeddings. In this section we will use the word2vec embeddings, which were trained on the Google News corpus. This corpus contains more than one hundred billion words, and word2vec contains 300-dimensional vectors for more than three million English words. We will also use the Python library gensim to inspect the model, measure the similarity of words, and complete analogies. In later chapters we will use these representations as features:

```
# In[1]:
# See https://radimrehurek.com/gensim/install.html for gensim
    installatio instructions
# Download and gunzip the word2vec embeddings from
#
https://drive.google.com/file/d/0B7XkCwpI5KDYNlNUTT1SS21pQmM/edit?usp=shari
ng
# The 1.5GB compressed file decompresses to 3.4GB.
import gensim

# The model is large; >= 8GB of RAM is required
model = gensim.models.KeyedVectors.load_word2vec_format('./GoogleNews-
    vectors- negative300.bin', binary=True)

# Let's inspect the embedding for "cat"
embedding = model.word_vec('cat')
print("Dimensions: %s" % embedding.shape)
print(embedding)

# Out[2]:
Dimensions: 300
[ 0.0123291 0.20410156 -0.28515625 0.21679688 0.11816406 0.08300781
  0.04980469 -0.00952148 0.22070312 -0.12597656 0.08056641 -0.5859375
  -0.00445557 -0.296875 -0.01312256 -0.08349609 0.05053711 0.15136719
  -0.44921875 -0.0135498 0.21484375 -0.14746094 0.22460938 -0.125
  -0.09716797 0.24902344 -0.2890625 0.36523438 0.41210938 -0.0859375
  -0.07861328 -0.19726562 -0.09082031 -0.14160156 -0.10253906 0.13085938
```

```
-0.00346375 0.07226562 0.04418945 0.34570312 0.07470703 -0.11230469
0.06738281 0.11230469 0.01977539 -0.12353516 0.20996094 -0.07226562
-0.02783203 0.05541992 -0.33398438 0.08544922 0.34375 0.13964844
0.04931641 -0.13476562 0.16308594 -0.37304688 0.39648438 0.10693359
0.22167969 0.21289062 -0.08984375 0.20703125 0.08935547 -0.08251953
0.05957031 0.10205078 -0.19238281 -0.09082031 0.4921875 0.03955078
-0.07080078 -0.0019989 -0.23046875 0.25585938 0.08984375 -0.10644531
0.00105286 -0.05883789 0.05102539 -0.0291748 0.19335938 -0.14160156
-0.33398438 0.08154297 -0.27539062 0.10058594 -0.10449219 -0.12353516
-0.140625 0.03491211 -0.11767578 -0.1796875 -0.21484375 -0.23828125
0.08447266 -0.07519531 -0.25976562 -0.21289062 -0.22363281 -0.09716797
0.11572266 0.15429688 0.07373047 -0.27539062 0.14257812 -0.0201416
0.10009766 -0.19042969 -0.09375 0.14160156 0.17089844 0.3125
-0.16699219 -0.08691406 -0.05004883 -0.24902344 -0.20800781 -0.09423828
-0.12255859 -0.09472656 -0.390625 -0.06640625 -0.31640625 0.10986328
-0.00156403 0.04345703 0.15625 -0.18945312 -0.03491211 0.03393555
-0.14453125 0.01611328 -0.14160156 -0.02392578 0.01501465 0.07568359
0.10742188 0.12695312 0.10693359 -0.01184082 -0.24023438 0.0291748
0.16210938 0.19921875 -0.28125 0.16699219 -0.11621094 -0.25585938
0.38671875 -0.06640625 -0.4609375 -0.06176758 -0.14453125 -0.11621094
0.05688477 0.03588867 -0.10693359 0.18847656 -0.16699219 -0.01794434
0.10986328 -0.12353516 -0.16308594 -0.14453125 0.12890625 0.11523438
0.13671875 0.05688477 -0.08105469 -0.06152344 -0.06689453 0.27929688
-0.19628906 0.07226562 0.12304688 -0.20996094 -0.22070312 0.21386719
-0.1484375 -0.05932617 0.05224609 0.06445312 -0.02636719 0.13183594
0.19433594 0.27148438 0.18652344 0.140625 0.06542969 -0.14453125
0.05029297 0.08837891 0.12255859 0.26757812 0.0534668 -0.32226562
-0.20703125 0.18164062 0.04418945 -0.22167969 -0.13769531 -0.04174805
-0.00286865 0.04077148 0.07275391 -0.08300781 0.08398438 -0.3359375
-0.40039062 0.01757812 -0.18652344 -0.0480957 -0.19140625 0.10107422
0.09277344 -0.30664062 -0.19921875 -0.0168457 0.12207031 0.14648438
-0.12890625 -0.23535156 -0.05371094 -0.06640625 0.06884766 -0.03637695
0.2109375 -0.06005859 0.19335938 0.05151367 -0.05322266 0.02893066
-0.27539062 0.08447266 0.328125 0.01818848 0.01495361 0.04711914
0.37695312 -0.21875 -0.03393555 0.01116943 0.36914062 0.02160645
0.03466797 0.07275391 0.16015625 -0.16503906 -0.296875 0.15039062
-0.29101562 0.13964844 0.00448608 0.171875 -0.21972656 0.09326172
-0.19042969 0.01599121 -0.09228516 0.15722656 -0.14160156 -0.0534668
0.03613281 0.23632812 -0.15136719 -0.00689697 -0.27148438 -0.07128906
-0.16503906 0.18457031 -0.08398438 0.18554688 0.11669922 0.02758789
-0.04760742 0.17871094 0.06542969 -0.03540039 0.22949219 0.02697754
-0.09765625 0.26953125 0.08349609 -0.13085938 -0.10107422 -0.00738525
0.07128906 0.14941406 -0.20605469 0.18066406 -0.15820312 0.05932617
0.28710938 -0.04663086 0.15136719 0.4921875 -0.27539062 0.05615234]

# In[2]:
# The vectors for semantically similar words are more similar than the
  vectors for semantically dissimilar words
```

```
print(model.similarity('cat', 'dog'))
print(model.similarity('cat', 'sandwich'))

# Out[2]:
0.760945708978
0.172112036738

# In[3]:
# Puppy is to cat as kitten is to...
print(model.most_similar(positive=['puppy', 'cat'], negative=['kitten'],
topn=1))

# Out[3]:
[(u'dog', 0.7762665152549744)]

# In[4]:
# Palette is to painter as saddle is to...
for i in model.most_similar(positive=['saddle', 'painter'], negative=
  ['palette'], topn=3):
    print(i)

# Out[4]:
(u'saddles', 0.5282258987426758)
(u'horseman', 0.5179383158683777)
(u'jockey', 0.48861297965049744)
```

Extracting features from images

Computer vision is the study and design of computational artifacts for processing and understanding images. These artifacts sometimes employ machine learning. An overview of computer vision is far beyond the scope of this book, but in this section, we will review some basic techniques used in computer vision for representing images in machine learning problems.

Extracting features from pixel intensities

A digital image is usually a raster, or pixmap, that maps colors to coordinates on a grid. That is, an image can be viewed as a matrix in which each element represents a color. A basic feature representation for an image can be constructed by reshaping the matrix into a vector by concatenating its rows together. **Optical Character Recognition (OCR)** is a canonical machine learning problem. Let's use this technique to create basic feature representations that can be used in an OCR application to recognize hand-written digits in character-delimited forms.

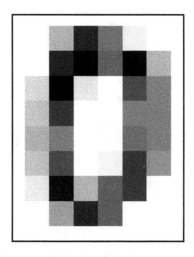

The `digits` dataset included with scikit-learn contains grayscale images of more than *1700* hand-written digits between zero and nine. Each image has eight pixels on a side. Each pixel is represented by an intensity value between *0* and *16*; white is the most intense and is indicated by 0, and black is the least intense and is indicated by *16*. The previous figure is an image of a hand-written digit taken from the dataset. Let's create a feature vector for the image by reshaping its matrix into a 64-dimensional vector:

```
# In[1]:
from sklearn import datasets

digits = datasets.load_digits()
print('Digit: %s' % digits.target[0])
print(digits.images[0])
print('Feature vector:\n %s' % digits.images[0].reshape(-1, 64))

# Out[1]:
Digit: 0
[[  0.   0.   5.  13.   9.   1.   0.   0.]
 [  0.   0.  13.  15.  10.  15.   5.   0.]
```

```
[  0.   3.  15.   2.   0.  11.   8.   0.]
[  0.   4.  12.   0.   0.   8.   8.   0.]
[  0.   5.   8.   0.   0.   9.   8.   0.]
[  0.   4.  11.   0.   1.  12.   7.   0.]
[  0.   2.  14.   5.  10.  12.   0.   0.]
[  0.   0.   6.  13.  10.   0.   0.   0.]]
Feature vector:
[[  0.   0.   5.  13.   9.   1.   0.   0.   0.   0.  13.  15.  10.
   15.
    5.   0.   0.   3.  15.   2.   0.  11.   8.   0.   0.   4.  12.   0.
    0.   8.   8.   0.   0.   5.   8.   0.   0.   9.   8.   0.   0.   4.
   11.   0.   1.  12.   7.   0.   0.   2.  14.   5.  10.  12.   0.   0.
    0.   0.   6.  13.  10.   0.   0.   0.]]
```

This representation can be effective for some basic tasks, like recognizing printed characters. However, recording the intensity of every pixel in the image produces prohibitively large feature vectors. A tiny *100 x 100* pixel grayscale image would require a *10,000*-dimensional vector, and a *1920 x 1080* pixel grayscale image would require a *2,073,600*-dimensional vector. Unlike the tf-idf feature vectors we created, in most problems, these vectors are not sparse. Space complexity is not the only disadvantage of this representation; learning from the intensities of pixels at particular locations results in models that are sensitive to changes in the scale, rotation, and translation of images. A model trained on our basic feature representations might not be able to recognize the same zero if it were shifted a few pixels in any direction, enlarged, or rotated a few degrees. Furthermore, learning from pixel intensities is itself problematic, as the model can become sensitive to changes in illumination. For these reasons, this representation is ineffective for tasks that involve photographs or other natural images. Modern computer vision applications frequently either use hand-engineered feature extraction methods that are applicable to many different problems, or automatically learn features without any supervision problem using techniques such as **deep learning**. We will focus on the latter in the next section.

Using convolutional neural network activations as features

In recent years, **convolutional neural networks** (**CNNs**) have been successfully applied to a variety of tasks, including computer vision tasks such as object recognition and semantic segmentation. We will not discuss CNN in detail in this section; while we will discuss ordinary neural networks like multi-layer perceptrons in a later chapter, scikit-learn is not suitable for deep learning.

As in the word embeddings section, we are interested in CNNs only to use them to extract features to use in other models. We will use the Python bindings for Caffe, a popular deep learning library, and a pre-trained network called **CaffeNet** to extract features from images. As with word embeddings, we will use a representation created by a model that was trained for a different task. In this case, the CaffeNet was trained to recognize *1,000* classes of objects. The classes include animals, vehicles, and household goods; see `http://image-n et.org/challenges/LSVRC/2014/browse-synsets`for a complete list of the classes. We will use the activations, or output, of the second-to-last layer of CaffeNet. This *4,096*-dimensional vector represents images in a metric space, and is invariant to image translations, rotations, and changes in illumination. Similar vectors should represent images that are semantically similar, even if their pixel intensities are different.

See `http://caffe.berkeleyvision.org/installation.html`for installation instructions for Windows, Mac OS, and Ubuntu. We require both Caffe and its Python library. Append the path to the `caffe/python` directory to your `PYTHONPATH` environment variable, and follow the instructions at `http://caffe.berkeleyvision.org/gathered/examples/image net.html`to download CaffeNet. Let's extract features from the following image:

The following script loads the model, pre-processes the image, and propagates the input forward through the network.

```
# In[1]:
import os
import caffe
import numpy as np
```

```
CAFFE_DIR = '/your/path/to/caffe'
MEAN_PATH = os.path.join(CAFFE_DIR,
   'python/caffe/imagenet/ilsvrc_2012_mean.npy')
PROTOTXT_PATH = os.path.join(CAFFE_DIR,
   'models/bvlc_reference_caffenet/deploy.prototxt')
CAFFEMODEL_PATH = os.path.join(CAFFE_DIR,
   'models/bvlc_reference_caffenet/bvlc_reference_caffenet.caffemodel')
IMAGE_PATH = 'data/zipper-1.jpg'

# Initialize the network
net = caffe.Net(PROTOTXT_PATH, CAFFEMODEL_PATH, caffe.TEST)
# Configure a Transformer to process an input image by scaling its values
to the range [0, 1], subtracting the per-channel pixel means,
   and transposing the channels to BGR color space.
# Test images must be preprocessed in the same way as training images.
transformer = caffe.io.Transformer({'data':
   net.blobs['data'].data.shape})
transformer.set_transpose('data', (2, 0, 1))
transformer.set_mean('data', np.load(MEAN_PATH).mean(1).mean(1))
transformer.set_raw_scale('data', 255)
transformer.set_channel_swap('data', (2,1,0))

# Load an image
net.blobs['data'].reshape(1, 3, 227, 227)
net.blobs['data'].data[0] = transformer.preprocess('data',
   caffe.io.load_image(IMAGE_PATH))

# Forward propagate and print the activations of the "fc7" layer.
net.forward()
features = net.blobs['fc7'].data.reshape(-1,)
print(features.shape)
print(features)

# Out[1]:
(4096,)
[ 0.          0.          0.77542615 ...,  0.          0.          0.
]
```

Summary

In this chapter, we discussed feature extraction. We learned several techniques for creating representations of data that can be used by machine learning algorithms. First, we created features from categorical explanatory variables using one-hot encoding and scikit-learn's DictVectorizer. We learned to standardize data to ensure that our estimators can learn from all of the features and can converge as quickly as possible.

Second, we extracted features from one of the most common types of data used in machine learning problems: text. We worked through several variations of the bag-of-words model, which discards all syntax and encodes only the frequencies of the tokens in a document. We began by creating basic binary term frequencies with `CountVectorizer`. We learned to preprocess text by filtering stop-words and stemming tokens, and replaced the term counts in our feature vectors with tf-idf weights that penalize common words and normalize for documents of different lengths. We then discussed word embeddings, which represent words using vectors instead of scalars.

Third, we extracted features from images. We began by representing images of hand-written digits with flattened matrices of pixel intensities. We then used the activations of a pre-trained CNN as lower-dimensional feature representations. These representations are invariant to image translations, rotations, and changes in illumination, and will allow our models to generalize more efficiently. We will use these feature extraction techniques in the subsequent chapters' examples.

5
From Simple Linear Regression to Multiple Linear Regression

In `Chapter 2`, *Simple Linear Regression* we used simple linear regression to model the relationship between a single explanatory variable and a continuous response variable; we used the diameter of a pizza to predict its price. In `Chapter 3`, *Classification and Regression with K-Nearest Neighbors* we introduced KNN and trained classifiers and regressors that used more than one explanatory variable to make predictions. In this chapter, we will discuss a multiple linear regression, a generalization of simple linear regression that regresses a continuous response variable onto multiple features. We will first analytically solve the values of the parameters that minimize the RSS cost function. We will then introduce a powerful learning algorithm that can estimate the values of the parameters that minimize a variety of cost functions, called **gradient descent**. We will discuss polynomial regression, another special case of multiple linear regression, and learn why increasing the model's complexity can increase the risk that it fails to generalize.

Multiple linear regression

We previously trained and evaluated a model for predicting the price of a pizza. While you are eager to demonstrate the pizza price predictor to your friends and coworkers, you are concerned by the model's imperfect R-squared score and the embarrassment its predictions could cause you. How can you improve the model?

Recalling your personal pizza-eating experience; you might have some intuitions about other attributes of a pizza that are related to its price. For instance, the price often depends on the number of toppings on the pizza. Fortunately, your pizza journal describes toppings in detail; let's add the number of toppings to our training data as a second explanatory variable. We cannot proceed with simple linear regression, but we can use a generalization of simple linear regression that can use multiple explanatory variables called **multiple linear regression**. Multiple linear regression is given by the following model:

$$y = \alpha + \beta_1 x_1 + \beta_2 x_2 + \cdots + \beta_n x_n$$

Whereas simple linear regression uses a single explanatory variable with a single coefficient, multiple linear regression uses a coefficient for each of an arbitrary number of explanatory variables. The model for linear regression can also be written in vector notation as:

$$Y = X\beta$$

This vector notation is equivalent to the following for simple linear regression:

$$\begin{bmatrix} Y_1 \\ Y_2 \\ \vdots \\ Y_n \end{bmatrix} = \begin{bmatrix} \alpha + \beta X_1 \\ \alpha + \beta X_2 \\ \vdots \\ \alpha + \beta X_n \end{bmatrix} = \begin{bmatrix} 1 & X_1 \\ 1 & X_2 \\ \vdots & \vdots \\ 1 & X_n \end{bmatrix} \times \begin{bmatrix} \alpha \\ \beta \end{bmatrix}$$

y is a column vector of values of the response variables for the training examples. β is a column vector of the values of the model's parameters. X, which is sometimes called the **design matrix**, is an m by n dimensional matrix of the values of the explanatory variables for the training examples. m is the number of training examples, and n is the number of features. Let's update our pizza training data to include the number of toppings:

Training example	Diameter in inches	Number of toppings	Price in dollars
1	6	2	7
2	8	1	9
3	10	0	13
4	14	2	17.5
5	18	0	18

We must also update our test data to include the second explanatory variable:

Test instance	Diameter in inches	Number of toppings	Price in dollars
1	8	2	11
2	9	0	8.5
3	11	2	15
4	16	2	18
5	12	0	11

Our learning algorithm must estimate the values of three parameters: the coefficients for the two features and the intercept term. While one might be tempted to solve for Beta by dividing each side of the equation by X, recall that division by a matrix is impossible. However, just as dividing by an integer is equivalent to multiplying by the inverse of the same integer, we can multiply by the inverse of X to avoid matrix division. A caveat is that only square matrices can be inverted. X is almost certainly not square; and we can't allow the number of features to constrain the number of training instances. To avoid this constraint, we will multiply X by its transpose to yield a square matrix that can be inverted. Denoted with a superscript T, the transpose of a matrix is formed by turning the rows of the matrix into columns and vice versa, as follows:

$$\begin{bmatrix} 1 & 2 & 3 \\ 4 & 5 & 6 \end{bmatrix}^T = \begin{bmatrix} 1 & 4 \\ 2 & 5 \\ 3 & 6 \end{bmatrix}$$

To recap, our model is given by the following:

$$Y = X\beta$$

We know the values of Y and X from our training data. We must find the values of Beta that minimize the cost function. We can analytically solve for Beta as follows:

$$\beta = (X^T X)^{-1} X^T Y$$

We can solve for Beta using NumPy, as follows:

```
# In[1]:
from numpy.linalg import inv
from numpy import dot, transpose

X = [[1, 6, 2], [1, 8, 1], [1, 10, 0], [1, 14, 2], [1, 18, 0]]
y = [[7], [9], [13], [17.5], [18]]
print(dot(inv(dot(transpose(X), X)), dot(transpose(X), y)))

# Out[1]:
[[ 1.1875    ]
 [ 1.01041667]
 [ 0.39583333]]
```

NumPy also provides a least squares function that can solve for the values of the parameters more compactly:

```
# In[1]:
from numpy.linalg import lstsq

X = [[1, 6, 2], [1, 8, 1], [1, 10, 0], [1, 14, 2], [1, 18, 0]]
y = [[7], [9], [13], [17.5], [18]]
print(lstsq(X, y)[0])

# Out[1]:
[[ 1.1875    ]
 [ 1.01041667]
 [ 0.39583333]]
```

Let's update our pizza price predictor program to use the second explanatory variable and compare its performance on the test set to that of the simple linear regression model:

```
# In[1]:
from sklearn.linear_model import LinearRegression

X = [[6, 2], [8, 1], [10, 0], [14, 2], [18, 0]]
y = [[7], [9], [13], [17.5], [18]]
model = LinearRegression()
model.fit(X, y)
X_test = [[8, 2], [9, 0], [11, 2], [16, 2], [12, 0]]
y_test = [[11], [8.5], [15], [18], [11]]
predictions = model.predict(X_test)
for i, prediction in enumerate(predictions):
    print('Predicted: %s, Target: %s' % (prediction, y_test[i]))
    print('R-squared: %.2f' % model.score(X_test, y_test))

# Out[1]:
```

```
Predicted: [ 10.0625], Target: [11]
R-squared: 0.77
Predicted: [ 10.28125], Target: [8.5]
R-squared: 0.77
Predicted: [ 13.09375], Target: [15]
R-squared: 0.77
Predicted: [ 18.14583333], Target: [18]
R-squared: 0.77
Predicted: [ 13.3125], Target: [11]
R-squared: 0.77
```

It appears that adding the number of toppings as an explanatory variable has improved the performance of our model. In later sections, we will discuss why evaluating a model on a single test set can provide inaccurate estimates of the model's performance, and how we can estimate the performance of our model more accurately by training and testing on many partitions of the data. For now, however, we can accept that the multiple linear regression model performs better than the simple linear regression model. There may be other attributes of pizzas that can be used to explain their prices. What if the relationship between these explanatory variables and the response variable is not linear in the real world? In the next section, we will examine a special case of multiple linear regression that can be used to model non-linear relationships.

Polynomial regression

In the previous examples, we assumed that the real relationship between the explanatory variables and the response variable is linear. In this section, we will use polynomial regression, a special case of multiple linear regression that models a linear relationship between the response variable and polynomial feature terms. The real-world curvilinear relationship is captured by transforming the features, which are then fit in the same manner as in multiple linear regression. For ease of visualization, we will again use only one explanatory variable, the pizza's diameter, in this section. Let's compare linear regression with polynomial regression using the following datasets:

Training instance	Diameter in inches	Price in dollars
1	6	7
2	8	9
3	10	13
4	14	17.5
5	18	18

Testing instance	Diameter in inches	Price in dollars
1	6	7
2	8	9
3	10	13
4	14	17.5

Quadratic regression, or regression with a second-order polynomial, is given by the following:

$$y = \alpha + \beta_1 x + \beta_2 x^2$$

Note that we are using only one feature for one explanatory variable, but the model now has three terms instead of two. The explanatory variable has been transformed and added as a third term to the model to capture the curvilinear relationship. Also note that the equation for polynomial regression is the same as the equation for multiple linear regression in vector notation. The PolynomialFeatures transformer can be used to easily add polynomial features to a feature representation. Let's fit a model to these features and compare it to the simple linear regression model:

```
# In[1]:
import numpy as np
import matplotlib.pyplot as plt
from sklearn.linear_model import LinearRegression
from sklearn.preprocessing import PolynomialFeatures

X_train = [[6], [8], [10], [14], [18]]
y_train = [[7], [9], [13], [17.5], [18]]
X_test = [[6], [8], [11], [16]]
y_test = [[8], [12], [15], [18]]
regressor = LinearRegression()
regressor.fit(X_train, y_train)
xx = np.linspace(0, 26, 100)
yy = regressor.predict(xx.reshape(xx.shape[0], 1))
plt.plot(xx, yy)
quadratic_featurizer = PolynomialFeatures(degree=2)
X_train_quadratic = quadratic_featurizer.fit_transform(X_train)
X_test_quadratic = quadratic_featurizer.transform(X_test)
regressor_quadratic = LinearRegression()
regressor_quadratic.fit(X_train_quadratic, y_train)
xx_quadratic = quadratic_featurizer.transform(xx.reshape(xx.shape[0], 1))
plt.plot(xx, regressor_quadratic.predict(xx_quadratic), c='r', linestyle='-
-')
```

```
plt.title('Pizza price regressed on diameter')
plt.xlabel('Diameter in inches')
plt.ylabel('Price in dollars')
plt.axis([0, 25, 0, 25])
plt.grid(True)
plt.scatter(X_train, y_train)
plt.show()
print(X_train)
print(X_train_quadratic)
print(X_test)
print(X_test_quadratic)
print('Simple linear regression r-squared', regressor.score(X_test,
y_test))
print('Quadratic regression r-squared',
  regressor_quadratic.score(X_test_quadratic, y_test))

# Out[1]:
[[6], [8], [10], [14], [18]]
[[   1.    6.    36.]
 [   1.    8.    64.]
 [   1.   10.   100.]
 [   1.   14.   196.]
 [   1.   18.   324.]]
[[6], [8], [11], [16]]
[[   1.    6.    36.]
 [   1.    8.    64.]
 [   1.   11.   121.]
 [   1.   16.   256.]]
('Simple linear regression r-squared', 0.80972679770766498)
('Quadratic regression r-squared', 0.86754436563450898)
```

The simple linear regression model is plotted with the solid line. Plotted with a dashed line, the quadratic regression model visibly fits the training data better:

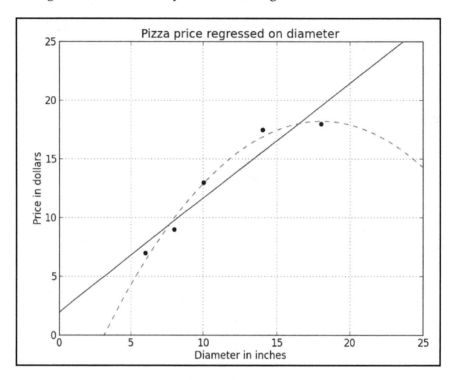

The R-squared score of the simple linear regression model is *0.81*; the quadratic regression model's R-squared score is an improvement at *0.87*. While quadratic and cubic regression models are the most common, we can add polynomials of any degree. The following figure plots the quadratic and cubic models:

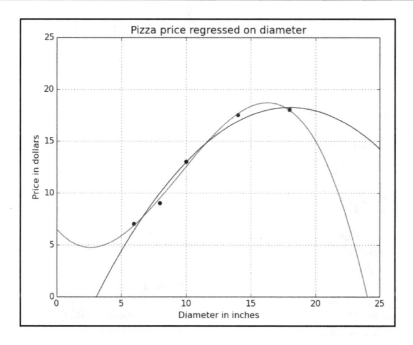

Now let's try an even higher order polynomial. The plot in the following figure shows a regression curve created by a ninth-degree polynomial:

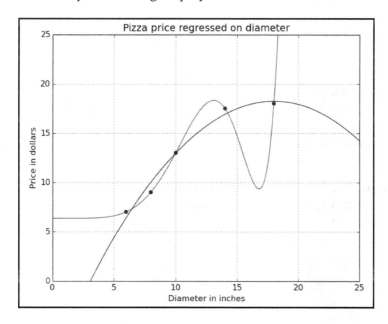

The model fits the training data almost exactly! The model's R-squared score on the test set, however, is *-0.09*. We have learned an extremely complex model that fits the training data exactly, but fails to approximate the real relationship. This problem is called **overfitting**. The model should induce a general rule for mapping inputs to outputs; instead, it has memorized the inputs and outputs from the training data. As a result, the model performs poorly on test data. This model predicts that a *16*-inch pizza should cost less than *$10*, while an *18*-inch pizza should cost more than *$30*. This model exactly fits the training data, but failed to learn the real relationship between size and price.

Regularization

Regularization is a collection of techniques that can be used to prevent overfitting. Regularization adds information, often in the form of a penalty against complexity, to a problem. Occam's razor states that the hypothesis with the fewest assumptions is best. Accordingly, regularization attempts to find the simplest model that explains the data.

scikit-learn provides several regularized linear regression models. Ridge regression, also known as **Tikhonov regularization**, penalizes model parameters that become too large. Ridge regression modifies the RSS cost function by adding the L^2 norm of the coefficients, as follows:

$$RSS_{\text{ridge}} = \sum_{i=1}^{n}(y_i - x_i^T \beta)^2 + \lambda \sum_{j=1}^{p} \beta_j^2$$

Lambda is a hyperparameter that controls the strength of the penalty. Recall from `Chapter 3`, *Classification and Regression with K-Nearest Neighbors*, that hyperparameters are parameters of the model that control how the learning algorithm learns. As lambda increases, the penalty increases, and the value of the cost function increases. When lambda is equal to zero, ridge regression is equal to linear regression.

scikit-learn also provides an implementation of the **Least Absolute Shrinkage and Selection Operator** (**LASSO**). The LASSO penalizes the coefficients by adding their L^1 norm to the cost function, as follows:

$$RSS_{\text{lasso}} = \sum_{i=1}^{n}(y_i - x_i^T \beta)^2 + \lambda \sum_{j=1}^{p} \beta_j$$

The LASSO produces sparse parameters; most of the coefficients will become zero, and the model will depend on a small subset of the features. In contrast, ridge regression produces models in which most parameters are small but non-zero. When explanatory variables are correlated, the LASSO will shrink the coefficients of one variable towards zero. Ridge regression will shrink them more uniformly.

Finally, scikit-learn provides an implementation of elastic net regularization, which linearly combines the L^1 and L^2 penalties used by the LASSO and ridge regression. That is, LASSO and ridge regression are both special cases of the elastic net method in which the hyperparameter for either the L^1 or L^2 penalty is equal to zero.

Applying linear regression

We have worked through a toy problem to learn how linear regression models relationships between explanatory and response variables. Now we'll use a real dataset and apply linear regression to an important task. Assume that you are at a party, and that you wish to drink the best wine that is available. You could ask your friends for recommendations, but you suspect that they will drink anything, regardless of its provenance. Fortunately, you have brought pH test strips and other tools for measuring various physicochemical properties—it is, after all, a party. We will use machine learning to predict the quality of wine based on its physicochemical attributes.

The **UCI Machine Learning Repository's** Wine dataset measures eleven physicochemical attributes, including pH and alcohol content, of *1,599* different red wines. Each wine's quality has been scored by human judges. The scores range from zero to ten; zero is the worst quality, and ten is the best quality. The dataset can be downloaded from `https://arc hive.ics.uci.edu/ml/datasets/Wine`. We will approach this problem as a regression task and regress the wine's quality onto one or more physicochemical attributes. The response variable in this problem takes only integer values between *0* and *10*; we could view these as discrete values and approach the problem as a multi-class classification task. In this chapter, however, we will pretend that the ratings are continuous.

Exploring the data

The training data contains the following explanatory variables: fixed acidity, volatile acidity, citric acid, residual sugar, chlorides, free sulfur dioxide, total sulfur dioxide, density, pH, sulphates, and alcohol content. Understanding these attributes could provide some insight as to the design of the model, and domain expertise is often important to designing successful machine learning systems. For this example, it is not necessary to be able to interpret the effects of the physicochemical attributes on the quality of wine, and the explanatory variables' units will be omitted for brevity. Let's examine a sample of the training data:

Fixed acidity	Volatile acidity	Citric acid	Residual sugar	Chlorides	Free sulfur dioxide	Total sulfur dioxide	Density	pH	Sulphates	Alcohol	Quality
7.4	0.7	0	1.9	0.076	11	34	0.9978	3.51	0.56	9.4	5
7.8	0.88	0	2.6	0.098	25	67	0.9968	3.2	0.68	9.8	5
7.8	0.76	0.04	2.3	0.092	15	54	0.997	3.26	0.65	9.8	5
11.2	0.28	0.56	1.9	0.075	17	60	0.998	3.16	0.58	9.8	6

scikit-learn is intended to be a tool for building machine learning systems, and it has fewer capabilities for exploring data than other packages. We will use pandas, an open source data analysis library for Python, to generate descriptive statistics from the data; we will use these statistics to inform some of the design decisions for our model. pandas introduces Python to some concepts from the R language, such as the dataframe, a two-dimensional, tabular, and heterogeneous data structure. Using pandas for data analysis is itself the topic of several books; we will use only a few basic methods in the following examples.

First, we will load the dataset and review some basic summary statistics for the variables. The data is provided as a `.csv` file. Note that the fields are delimited by semicolons rather than commas:

```
# In[1]:
import pandas as pd

df = pd.read_csv('./winequality-red.csv', sep=';')
df.describe()
```

	Fixed acidity	Volatile acidity	Citric acid	Residual sugar	Chlorides	Free sulfur dioxide	Total sulfur dioxide	Density	pH	Sulphates	Alcohol	Quality
Count	1599.000000	1599.000000	1599.000000	1599.000000	1599.000000	1599.000000	1599.000000	1599.000000	1599.000000	1599.000000	1599.000000	1599.000000
mean	8.319637	0.527821	0.270976	2.538806	0.087467	15.874922	46.467792	0.996747	3.311113	0.658149	10.422983	5.636023
std	1.741096	0.179060	0.194801	1.409928	0.047065	10.460157	32.895324	0.001887	0.154386	0.169507	1.065668	0.807569
min	4.600000	0.120000	0.000000	0.900000	0.012000	1.000000	6.000000	0.990070	2.740000	0.330000	8.400000	3.000000
25%	7.100000	0.390000	0.090000	1.900000	0.070000	7.000000	22.000000	0.995600	3.210000	0.550000	9.500000	5.000000
50%	7.900000	0.520000	0.260000	2.200000	0.079000	14.000000	38.000000	0.996750	3.310000	0.620000	10.200000	6.000000

| 75% | 9.200000 | 0.640000 | 0.420000 | 2.600000 | 0.090000 | 21.000000 | 62.000000 | 0.997835 | 3.400000 | 0.730000 | 11.100000 | 6.000000 |
| max | 15.900000 | 1.580000 | 1.000000 | 15.500000 | 0.611000 | 72.000000 | 289.000000 | 1.003690 | 4.010000 | 2.000000 | 14.900000 | 8.000000 |

The `pd.read_csv()` function is a convenience utility that loads the `.csv` into a dataframe. `Dataframe.describe()` calculates summary statistic for each column of the dataframe. The previous code sample shows the summary statistics for only the last four columns of the dataframe. Note the summary for the `quality` variable; most of the wines scored five or six. Visualizing the data can help indicate whether relationships exist between the response variable and the explanatory variables. Let's use `matplotlib` to create some scatter plots. The following snippet produces the next figure:

```
# In[2]:
import matplotlib.pylab as plt

plt.scatter(df['alcohol'], df['quality'])
plt.xlabel('Alcohol')
plt.ylabel('Quality')
plt.title('Alcohol Against Quality')
plt.show()
```

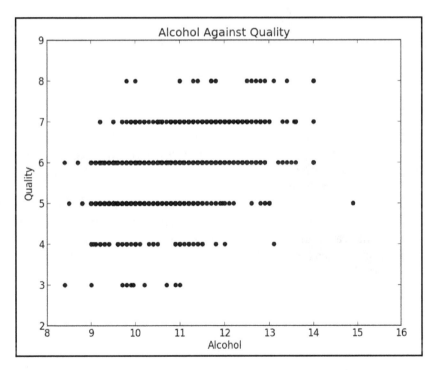

A weak positive relationship between **Alcohol** content and **Quality** is visible in the scatter plot in the previous figure; wines that have high alcohol content are often of high quality.

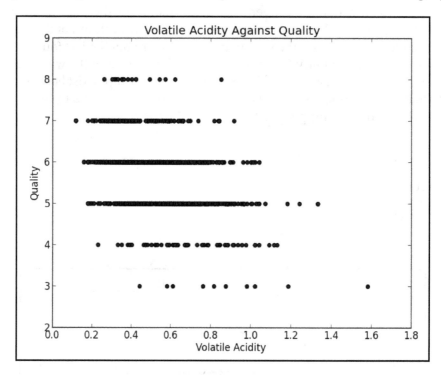

The previous figure reveals a negative relationship between **Volatile Acidity** and **Quality**. These plots suggest that the response variable depends on multiple explanatory variables; let's model the relationship with multiple linear regression. How can we decide which explanatory variables to include in the model? `Dataframe.corr()` calculates a pairwise correlation matrix. The correlation matrix confirms that the strongest positive correlation is between alcohol and quality, and that quality is strongly negatively correlated with volatile acidity, an attribute that can cause wine to taste like vinegar. To summarize, we have hypothesized that good wines have high alcohol contents and do not taste like vinegar. This hypothesis seems sensible, though it suggests that wine aficionados may have less sophisticated palates than they claim.

Fitting and evaluating the model

Now we will split the data into training and testing sets, train `regressor`, and evaluate its predictions:

```
# In[1]:
from sklearn.linear_model import LinearRegression
import pandas as pd
import matplotlib.pylab as plt
from sklearn.model_selection import train_test_split

df = pd.read_csv('./winequality-red.csv', sep=';')
X = df[list(df.columns)[:-1]]
y = df['quality']
X_train, X_test, y_train, y_test = train_test_split(X, y)
regressor = LinearRegression()
regressor.fit(X_train, y_train)
y_predictions = regressor.predict(X_test)
print('R-squared: %s' % regressor.score(X_test, y_test))

# Out[1]:
R-squared: 0.398550890379
```

First, we loaded the data using pandas, and separated the response variable from the explanatory variables. Next we used the function `train_test_split` to randomly partition the data into training and test sets. The proportions of the data for both partitions can be specified using keyword arguments. By default, *25 percent* of the data is assigned to the test set. Finally, we trained the model, and evaluated it on the test set. The R-squared score is *0.35*. The performance might change if a different *75 percent* of the data is partitioned to the training set. We can use cross validation to produce a better estimate of the estimator's performance. Recall from `Chapter 1`, *The Fundamentals of Machine Learning* that each cross validation round trains and tests different partitions of the data to reduce variability:

```
# In[1]:
import pandas as pd
from sklearn.model_selection import cross_val_score
from sklearn.linear_model import LinearRegression

df = pd.read_csv('./winequality-red.csv', sep=';')
X = df[list(df.columns)[:-1]]
y = df['quality']
regressor = LinearRegression()
scores = cross_val_score(regressor, X, y, cv=5)
print(scores.mean())
print(scores)
```

```
# Out[1]:
0.290041628842
[ 0.13200871  0.31858135  0.34955348  0.369145   0.2809196 ]
```

The `cross_val_score` helper function allows us to easily perform cross validation using the provided data and estimator. We specified five-fold cross validation using the `cv` keyword argument. That is, each instance will be randomly assigned to one of five partitions. Each partition will be used to train and test the model. The `cross_val_score` function returns the value of the estimator's score method for each round. The R-squared scores range from `0.13` to `0.36`! The mean of the scores, `0.29`, is a better estimate of the estimator's predictive power than the R-squared score produced from a single train/test split.

Let's inspect some of the model's predictions, and plot the true quality scores against the predicted scores:

```
Predicted: 4.89907499467 True: 4
Predicted: 5.60701048317 True: 6
Predicted: 5.92154439575 True: 6
Predicted: 5.54405696963 True: 5
Predicted: 6.07869910663 True: 7
Predicted: 6.036656327 True: 6
Predicted: 6.43923020473 True: 7
Predicted: 5.80270760407 True: 6
Predicted: 5.92425033278 True: 5
Predicted: 5.31809822449 True: 6
Predicted: 6.34837585295 True: 6
```

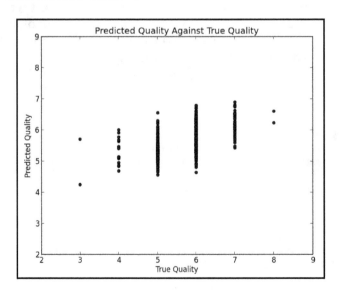

As expected, few predictions exactly match the true values of the response variable. The model is also better at predicting the qualities of average wines since most of the training data is for average wines.

Gradient descent

In the examples in this chapter, we analytically solved for the values of the model's parameters that minimize the cost function with the following equation:

$$\beta = (X^T X)^{-1} X^T Y$$

Recall that X is the matrix of features for each training example. The dot product of $X^T X$ results in a square matrix with dimensions n by n, where n is equal to the number of features. The computational complexity of inverting this square matrix is nearly cubic in the number of features. While the number of features has been small in this chapter's examples, this inversion can be prohibitively costly for problems with tens of thousands of explanatory variables, which we will encounter in the following chapters. Furthermore, it is impossible to invert X if its determinant is zero. In this section, we will discuss another method for efficiently estimating the optimal values of the model's parameters called **gradient descent**. Note that our definition of the goodness-of-fit has not changed; we will still use gradient descent to estimate the values of the model's parameters that minimize the value of the cost function.

Gradient descent is sometimes described by the analogy of a blindfolded person who is trying to find her way from somewhere on a mountainside to the lowest point of the valley. The person cannot see the topography, be she can judge the steepness of each step she takes. She takes a step in the direction with the steepest decline. She then takes another step, again in the direction with the steepest decline. The lengths of her strides are proportional to the steepness of the terrain at her current position. She takes big steps when the terrain is steep, as she is confident that she is still near the peak and that she will not overshoot the valley's lowest point. She takes smaller steps as the terrain becomes less steep. If she were to continue taking large steps, she may accidentally step over the valley's lowest point. She would then need to change direction and step toward the lowest point of the valley again. By taking decreasingly large steps she can avoid stepping back and forth over the valley's lowest point. The blindfolded person continues to walk until she cannot take a step that will decrease her altitude; at that point she has found the bottom of the valley.

Formally, gradient descent is an optimization algorithm that can be used to estimate the local minimum of a function. Recall that in our linear regression problems we are using the RSS cost function, which is given by the following equation:

$$SS_{res} = \sum_{i=1}^{n}(y_i - f(x_i))^2$$

We can use gradient descent to find the parameters that minimize a real-valued cost function, C, of many variables. Gradient descent iteratively updates the parameters by calculating the partial derivative of the cost function at each step. For this example, we will assume that C is a function of two variables v_1 and v_2. To minimize C using gradient descent, we need a small change in the variables to produce a small change in the output. Resuming our blind person analogy, we need to be able to take one step in the direction with the steepest descent at a time to reach the valley. We will represent a change in the value of v_1 with Δv_1, and a change in the value of v_2 with Δv_2. Taking a small step Δv_1 in the v_1 direction and Δv_2 in the v_2 direction results in a small change in the value of C, ΔC. More formally, we can relate the change in C to the changes in v_1 and v_2 with the following:

$$\Delta C \approx \frac{\partial C}{\partial v_1}\Delta v_1 + \frac{\partial C}{\partial v_2}\Delta v_2$$

Where $\partial C/\partial v_1$ is the partial derivative of C with respect to v_1. On each step, ΔC should be negative to decrease the cost. How do we choose Δv_1 and Δv_2? For convenience, we will represent $\Delta v1$ and $\Delta v2$ as vector:

$$\Delta v = \left(\Delta v_1, \Delta v_2\right)^T$$

We will also introduce the gradient vector of C:

$$\nabla C = \left(\frac{\partial C}{\partial v_1}, \frac{\partial C}{\partial v_2}\right)^T$$

We can therefore rewrite our formula for ΔC as the following:

$$\Delta C = \nabla C \Delta v$$

To guarantee that ΔC will be negative, we can set Δv to the following:

$$\Delta v = -\eta \nabla C$$

We will substitute for Δv in our formula for ΔC to make it more clear why ΔC will be negative:

$$\Delta C = -\eta \nabla C \cdot \nabla C$$

The ∇C squared will always be greater than zero. We then multiply it by a learning rate, η, and negate the product. On each iteration, we will calculate the gradient of C, and then subtract $\eta \nabla C$ from our variables vector to take a step in the direction of the steepest decline.

It is important to note that gradient descent estimates the local minimum of a function. Convex cost functions have a single minimum. A real-valued function is convex if a line segment between any two points on the graph of the function lies above or on the graph. A three-dimensional plot of the values of a convex cost function for all possible values of the parameters looks like a bowl. The bottom of the bowl is the minimum. Conversely, non-convex functions can have many local minimas. The plots of the values of their cost functions can have many peaks and valleys. Gradient descent is only guaranteed to find a local minimum; it will find a valley, but it will not necessarily find the lowest valley. Fortunately, the residual sum of squares cost function is convex.

An important hyperparameter of gradient descent is the learning rate, which controls the lengths of the blindfolded person's strides. If the learning rate is small enough, the cost function will decrease with each iteration until gradient descent has converged on the optimal parameters. As the learning rate decreases, however, the time required for gradient descent to converge increases; the blindfolded person will take longer to reach the valley if she takes small steps than if she takes large steps. If the learning rate is too large, she may repeatedly overstep the bottom of the valley; that is, gradient descent could oscillate around the optimal values of the parameters without converging.

Three varieties of gradient descent are distinguished by the number of training instances that are used to update the model parameters in each training iteration. **Batch gradient descent** uses all of the training instances to update the model parameters in each iteration. **Stochastic gradient descent**, in contrast, updates the parameters using only a single training instance in each iteration. The training instance is usually selected randomly. Both of these variants can be thought of as special cases of **mini-batch gradient descent**, which uses a batch of b training instances in each iteration.

Mini-batch or stochastic gradient descent are often preferred when there are hundreds of thousands of training instances or more, as they will converge more quickly than batch gradient descent. Batch gradient descent is a deterministic algorithm, and will produce the same parameter values given the same training set. As a stochastic algorithm, SGD can produce different parameter estimates each time it is run. Because it uses only single training instances to update the weights, SGD may not minimize the cost function as well as gradient descent. Its approximation is often close enough, particularly for convex cost functions like residual sum of squares.

Let's use stochastic gradient descent to estimate the parameters of a model with scikit-learn. `SGDRegressor` is an implementation of SGD that can be used even for regression problems with hundreds of thousands or more features. It can be used to optimize different cost functions to fit different models; by default, it will optimize RSS. In this example, we will predict the prices of houses from thirteen features:

```
# In[1]:
import numpy as np
from sklearn.datasets import load_boston
from sklearn.linear_model import SGDRegressor
from sklearn.model_selection import cross_val_score
from sklearn.preprocessing import StandardScaler
from sklearn.model_selection import train_test_split

data = load_boston()
X_train, X_test, y_train, y_test = train_test_split(data.data, data.target)
```

scikit-learn provides the `load_boston` convenience function for loading the dataset. First, we split the data into training and testing sets using `train_test_split`, and standardize the training data. Finally, we fit and evaluate the estimator:

```
# In[2]:
X_scaler = StandardScaler()
y_scaler = StandardScaler()
X_train = X_scaler.fit_transform(X_train)
y_train = y_scaler.fit_transform(y_train.reshape(-1, 1))
X_test = X_scaler.transform(X_test)
y_test = y_scaler.transform(y_test.reshape(-1, 1))
regressor = SGDRegressor(loss='squared_loss')
scores = cross_val_score(regressor, X_train, y_train, cv=5)
print('Cross validation r-squared scores: %s' % scores)
print('Average cross validation r-squared score: %s' % np.mean(scores))
regressor.fit(X_train, y_train)
print('Test set r-squared score %s' % regressor.score(X_test, y_test))

# Out[2]:
Cross validation r-squared scores: [ 0.55323539  0.77067053  0.78551352
```

```
0.69416906  0.53274918]
Average cross validation r-squared score: 0.667267533715
Test set r-squared score 0.733718249165
```

Summary

In this chapter, we introduced multiple linear regression, a generalization of simple linear regression that uses multiple features to predict the value of a response variable. We described polynomial regression, a linear model that can model non-linear relationships using polynomial feature terms. We introduced the concept of regularization, which can be used to prevent models from memorizing noise in the training data. Finally, we introduced gradient descent, a scalable learning algorithm that can estimate the parameter values that minimize a cost function.

6
From Linear Regression to Logistic Regression

In previous chapters, we discussed simple, multiple, and polynomial linear regression. The models are special cases of the **generalized linear model**, a flexible framework that requires fewer assumptions than ordinary linear regression. In this chapter, we will discuss some of these assumptions as they relate to another special case of the generalized linear model called **logistic regression**.

Unlike the regression models we have previously discussed, logistic regression is used for classification tasks. Recall that the goal in classification tasks is to induce a function that maps an observation to its associated class or label. A learning algorithm must use pairs of feature vectors and their corresponding labels to induce the values of the mapping function's parameters that produce the best classifier, as measured by some performance metric. In binary classification, the classifier must assign instances to one of two classes. In multi-class classification, the classifier must assign one of several labels to each instance. In multi-label classification, the classifier must assign a subset of the labels to each instance. In this chapter, we will work through several classification problems using logistic regression, discuss performance measures for the classification task, and apply some of the feature extraction techniques we learned in Chapter 4, *Feature Extraction*.

Binary classification with logistic regression

Ordinary linear regression assumes that the response variable is **normally distributed**. Normal distribution, or **Gaussian distribution**, is a function that describes the probability that an observation will have a value between any two real numbers. Normally distributed data is symmetrical; half of the values are greater than the mean and half of the values are less than the mean. The mean, median, and mode of normally distributed data are also equal. Many natural phenomena are approximately normally distributed. For instance, the height of people is normally distributed: most people are of average height, a few are tall, and a few are short. In some problems the response variable is not normally distributed. For instance, a coin toss can result in two outcomes: heads or tails. **Bernoulli distribution** describes the probability distribution of a random variable that can take the positive case with probability P or the negative case with probability $1 - P$. If the response variable represents a probability, it must be constrained to the range *[0, 1]*. Linear regression assumes that a constant change in the value of a feature results in a constant change in the value of the response variable, an assumption that cannot hold if the value of the response variable represents a probability. Generalized linear models remove this assumption by relating a linear combination of the features to the response variable using a link function. In fact, we've already used a link function in Chapter 2, *Simple Linear Regression*; ordinary linear regression is a special case of the generalized linear model that links a linear combination of the features to a normally distributed response variable using the identity function. We can use a different link function to relate a linear combination of the features to a response variable that is not normally distributed.

In logistic regression, the response variable describes the probability that the outcome is the positive case. If the response variable is equal to or exceeds a discrimination threshold, the positive class is predicted; otherwise, the negative class is predicted. The response variable is modeled as a function of a linear combination of the features using the **logistic function**. As illustrated by the following formula, the logistic function always returns a value between 0 and 1:

$$F(t) = \frac{1}{1 + e^{-t}}$$

e is a constant called **Euler's number**. It is an irrational number; the first few digits of it are *2.718*. The following is a plot of the value of the logistic function for the range *[-6, 6]*:

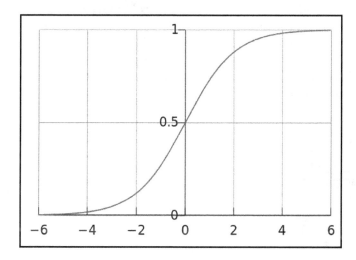

For logistic regression, *t* is equal to a linear combination of explanatory variables, as follows:

$$F(x) = \frac{1}{1 + e^{-(\beta_0 + \beta x)}}$$

The **logit** function is the inverse of the logistic function. It links *F(x)* back to a linear combination of the features, as follows:

$$g(x) = ln\frac{F(x)}{1 - F(x)} = \beta_0 + \beta x$$

The values of the model's parameters can be estimated using a variety of learning algorithms, including gradient descent. Now that we have defined the model for logistic regression, let's apply it to a binary classification task.

Spam filtering

Our first problem is a modern version of the canonical binary classification problem: spam filtering. In our version, however, we will classify spam and ham SMS messages rather than e-mail. We will extract tf-idf features from the messages using the techniques we learned in previous chapters, and classify the messages using logistic regression. We will use the **SMS Spam Collection Data Set** from the **UCI Machine Learning Repository**. The dataset can be downloaded from http://archive.ics.uci.edu/ml/datasets/SMS+Spam+Collection. First, let's explore the dataset and calculate some basic summary statistics using pandas:

```
# In[1]:
import pandas as pd
df = pd.read_csv('./SMSSpamCollection', delimiter='t', header=None)
print(df.head())

# Out[1]:
        0                                                              1
0    ham   Go until jurong point, crazy.. Available only ...
1    ham                       Ok lar... Joking wif u oni...
2   spam   Free entry in 2 a wkly comp to win FA Cup fina...
3    ham   U dun say so early hor... U c already then say...
4    ham   Nah I don't think he goes to usf, he lives aro...

# In[2]:
print('Number of spam messages: %s' % df[df[0] == 'spam'][0].count())
print('Number of ham messages: %s' % df[df[0] == 'ham'][0].count())

# Out[2]:
Number of spam messages: 747
Number of ham messages: 4825
```

Each row comprises a binary label and a text message. The dataset contains $5,574$ instances; 4827 messages are ham and the remaining 747 messages are spam. While the noteworthy, or case, outcome is often assigned the label 1 and the non-case outcome is often assigned 0, these assignments are arbitrary. Inspecting the data may reveal other attributes that should be captured in the model. The following selection of messages characterizes both the classes:

```
Spam: Free entry in 2 a wkly comp to win FA Cup final tkts 21st May 2005.
Text FA to 87121 to receive entry question(std txt rate)T&C's apply
08452810075over18's
Spam: WINNER!! As a valued network customer you have been selected to
receivea £900 prize reward! To claim call 09061701461. Claim code KL341.
Valid 12 hours only.
Ham: Sorry my roommates took forever, it ok if I come by now?
Ham: Finished class where are you.
```

Let's make some predictions using scikit-learn's `LogisticRegression` class. First, we split the dataset into training and test sets. By default, `train_test_split` assigns 75% of the samples to the training set and allocates the remaining 25% of the samples to the test set. Next, we create a `TfidfVectorizer`. Recall from Chapter 4, *Feature Extraction* that `TfidfVectorizer` combines `CountVectorizer` and `TfidfTransformer`. We fit it with the training messages and transform both the training and test messages. Finally, we create an instance of `LogisticRegression` and train the model. Like `LinearRegression`, `LogisticRegression` implements the `fit` and `predict` methods. As a sanity check, we've printed a few predictions for manual inspection:

```
# In[3]:
import numpy as np
import pandas as pd
from sklearn.feature_extraction.text import TfidfVectorizer
from sklearn.linear_model.logistic import LogisticRegression
from sklearn.model_selection import train_test_split, cross_val_score

X = df[1].values
y = df[0].values
X_train_raw, X_test_raw, y_train, y_test = train_test_split(X, y)
vectorizer = TfidfVectorizer()
X_train = vectorizer.fit_transform(X_train_raw)
X_test = vectorizer.transform(X_test_raw)
classifier = LogisticRegression()
classifier.fit(X_train, y_train)
predictions = classifier.predict(X_test)
for i, prediction in enumerate(predictions[:5]):
    print('Predicted: %s, message: %s' % (prediction,
        X_test_raw[i]))

# Out[3]:
Predicted: ham, message: Now thats going to ruin your thesis!
Predicted: ham, message: Ok...
Predicted: ham, message: Its a part of checking IQ
Predicted: spam, message: Ringtone Club: Gr8 new polys direct to your
mobile every week !
Predicted: ham, message: Talk sexy!! Make new friends or fall in love in
the worlds most discreet text dating service. Just text VIP to 83110 and
see who you could meet.
```

How well does our classifier perform? The performance metrics we used for linear regression are inappropriate for this task. We are interested only in whether the predicted class was correct, and not how far it was from the decision boundary. In the next section, we will discuss some performance metrics that can be used to evaluate binary classifiers.

Binary classification performance metrics

A variety of metrics exist for evaluating the performance of binary classifiers against trusted labels. The most common metrics are accuracy, precision, recall, F1 measure, and ROC AUC score. All of these measures depend on the concept of true positives, true negatives, false positives, and false negatives. Positive and negative refer to the classes. True and false denote whether the predicted class is the same as the true class.

For our SMS spam classifier, a true positive prediction is when the classifier correctly predicts that a message is spam. A true negative prediction is when the classifier correctly predicts that a message is ham. A prediction that a ham message is spam is a false positive prediction, and a spam message incorrectly classified as ham is a false negative prediction. A **confusion matrix**, or contingency table, can be used to visualize true and false positives and negatives. The rows of the matrix are the true classes of the instances, and the columns are the predicted classes of the instances:

```
# In[4]:
from sklearn.metrics import confusion_matrix
import matplotlib.pyplot as plt

y_test = [0, 0, 0, 0, 0, 1, 1, 1, 1, 1]
y_pred = [0, 1, 0, 0, 0, 0, 0, 1, 1, 1]
confusion_matrix = confusion_matrix(y_test, y_pred)
print(confusion_matrix)
plt.matshow(confusion_matrix)
plt.title('Confusion matrix')
plt.colorbar()
plt.ylabel('True label')
plt.xlabel('Predicted label')
plt.show()

# Out[4]:
[[4 1]
 [2 3]]
```

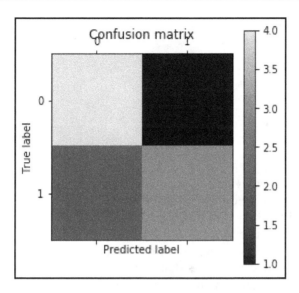

The **confusion matrix** indicates that there were four true negative predictions, three true positive predictions, two false negative predictions, and one false positive prediction. Confusion matrices become more useful in multi-class problems, in which it can be difficult to determine the most frequent types of errors.

Accuracy

Recall that accuracy measures the fraction of the classifier's predictions that are correct. `LogisticRegression.score` predicts and scores labels for a test set using accuracy. Let's evaluate our classifier's accuracy:

```
# In[1]:
import numpy as np
import pandas as pd
from sklearn.feature_extraction.text import TfidfVectorizer
from sklearn.linear_model.logistic import LogisticRegression
from sklearn.model_selection import train_test_split, cross_val_score
from sklearn.metrics import roc_curve, auc
import matplotlib.pyplot as plt

df = pd.read_csv('./sms.csv')
X_train_raw, X_test_raw, y_train, y_test =
  train_test_split(df['message'],
  df['label'], random_state=11)
vectorizer = TfidfVectorizer()
X_train = vectorizer.fit_transform(X_train_raw)
```

```
X_test = vectorizer.transform(X_test_raw)
classifier = LogisticRegression()
classifier.fit(X_train, y_train)
scores = cross_val_score(classifier, X_train, y_train, cv=5)
print('Accuracies: %s' % scores)
print('Mean accuracy: %s' % np.mean(scores))

# Out[1]:
Accuracies: [ 0.95221027  0.95454545  0.96172249  0.96052632  0.95209581]
Mean accuracy: 0.956220068309
```

While accuracy measures the overall correctness of the classifier, it does not distinguish between false positive errors and false negative errors. Some applications may be more sensitive to false negatives than false positives, or vice versa. Furthermore, accuracy is not an informative metric if the proportions of the classes are skewed in the population. For example, a classifier that predicts whether or not credit card transactions are fraudulent may be more sensitive to false negatives than to false positives. To promote customer satisfaction, the credit card company may prefer to risk verifying legitimate transactions rather than risk ignoring a fraudulent transaction. Because most transactions are legitimate, accuracy is not an appropriate metric for this problem. A classifier that always predicts that transactions are legitimate could have a high accuracy score but may not be useful. For these reasons, classifiers are often evaluated using precision and recall.

Precision and recall

Recall that precision is the fraction of positive predictions that are correct. In our SMS spam classifier, precision is the fraction of messages classified as spam that are actually spam. Sometimes called sensitivity in medical domains, recall is the fraction of the truly positive instances that the classifier recognized. A recall score of *1* indicates that the classifier did not make any false negative predictions. For our SMS spam classifier, recall is the fraction of truly spam messages that were classified as spam.

Individually, precision and recall are seldom informative; they are both incomplete views of a classifier's performance. Both precision and recall can fail to distinguish classifiers that perform well from certain types of classifiers that perform poorly. A trivial classifier could easily achieve a perfect recall score by predicting positive for every instance. For example, assume that a test set contains 10 positive examples and *10* negative examples. A classifier that predicts positive for every example will achieve a recall of *1*. A classifier that predicts negative for every example, or one that makes only false positive and true negative predictions, will achieve a recall score of *0*. Similarly, a classifier that predicts that only a single instance is positive and happens to be correct will achieve perfect precision. Let's calculate our SMS classifier's precision and recall:

```
# In[2]:
precisions = cross_val_score(classifier, X_train, y_train, cv=5,
    scoring='precision')
print('Precision: %s' % np.mean(precisions))
recalls = cross_val_score(classifier, X_train, y_train, cv=5,
    scoring='recall')
print('Recall: %s' % np.mean(recalls))

# Out[2]:
Precision: 0.992542742398
Recall: 0.683605030275
```

Our classifier's precision is 0.992; almost all of the messages that it predicted as spam were actually spam. Its recall is lower, indicating that it incorrectly classified approximately 32% of the spam messages as ham.

Calculating the F1 measure

The F1 measure is the harmonic mean of the precision and recall scores. The F1 measure penalizes classifiers with imbalanced precision and recall scores, like the trivial classifier that always predicts the positive class. A model with perfect precision and recall scores will achieve an F1 score of *1*. A model with a perfect precision score and a recall score of 0 will achieve an F1 score of *0*. Let's compute our classifier's F1 score:

```
# In[3]:
f1s = cross_val_score(classifier, X_train, y_train, cv=5,
    scoring='f1')
print('F1 score: %s' % np.mean(f1s))

# Out[3]:
F1 score: 0.809067846627
```

Models are sometimes evaluated using the F0.5 and F2 scores, which bias precision over recall and recall over precision, respectively.

ROC AUC

A **Receiver Operating Characteristic** (**ROC**) curve, visualizes a classifier's performance. Unlike accuracy, the ROC curve is insensitive to datasets with unbalanced class proportions; unlike precision and recall, the ROC curve illustrates the classifier's performance for all values of the discrimination threshold. ROC curves plot the classifier's recall against its **fall-out**. **Fall-out**, or the false positive rate, is the number of false positives divided by the total number of negatives. It is calculated using the following:

$$F = \frac{FP}{TN + FP}$$

AUC is the area under the ROC curve; it reduces the ROC curve to a single value that represents the expected performance of the classifier. The dashed line in the following figure is for a classifier that predicts classes randomly; it has an AUC of **0.5**. The solid curve is for a classifier that outperforms random guessing:

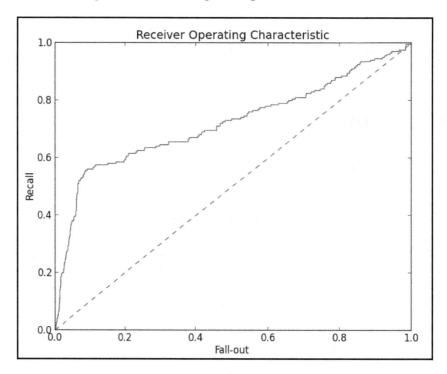

Let's plot the ROC curve for our SMS spam classifier:

```
# In[5]:
predictions = classifier.predict_proba(X_test)
false_positive_rate, recall, thresholds = roc_curve(y_test,
    predictions[:, 1])
roc_auc = auc(false_positive_rate, recall)
plt.title('Receiver Operating Characteristic')
plt.plot(false_positive_rate, recall, 'b', label='AUC = %0.2f' %
    roc_auc)
plt.legend(loc='lower right')
plt.plot([0, 1], [0, 1], 'r--')
plt.xlim([0.0, 1.0])
plt.ylim([0.0, 1.0])
plt.ylabel('Recall')
plt.xlabel('Fall-out')
plt.show()
```

From the ROC AUC plot it is apparent that our classifier outperforms random guessing; most of the area of the plot lies under its curve:

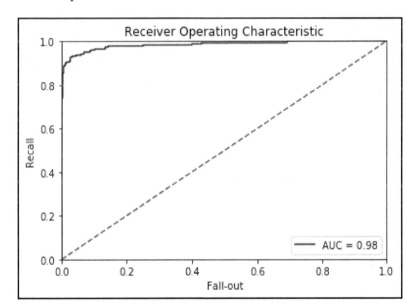

Tuning models with grid search

Recall from Chapter 3, *Classification and Regression with K-Nearest Neighbors* that hyperparameters are parameters of the model that the learning algorithm does not estimate. For example, hyperparameters of our logistic regression SMS classifier include the value of the regularization term and thresholds used to remove words that appear too frequently or infrequently. In scikit-learn, hyperparameters are set through the constructors of estimators and transformers. In the previous examples, we did not set any arguments for LogisticRegression; we used the default values for all of the hyperparameters. These default values are often a good start, but they may not produce the optimal model. **Grid search** is a common method for selecting the hyperparameter values that produce the best model. Grid search takes a set of possible values for each hyperparameter that should be tuned, and evaluates a model trained on each element of the Cartesian product of the sets. That is, grid search is an exhaustive search that trains and evaluates a model for each possible combination of the specified hyperparameter values. A disadvantage of grid search is that it is computationally costly for even small sets of hyperparameter values. Fortunately, it is an embarrassingly parallel problem; many models can easily be trained and evaluated concurrently since no synchronization is required between the processes. Let's use scikit-learn's GridSearchCV to find better hyperparameter values. GridSearchCV takes an estimator, a parameter space, and a performance measure. The n_jobs argument specifies the maximum number of concurrent jobs; set n_jobs to -1 to use all CPU cores. Note that fit must be called in a Python main block in order to fork additional processes:

```
# In[1]:
import pandas as pd
from sklearn.preprocessing import LabelEncoder
from sklearn.feature_extraction.text import TfidfVectorizer
from sklearn.linear_model.logistic import LogisticRegression
from sklearn.grid_search import GridSearchCV
from sklearn.pipeline import Pipeline
from sklearn.model_selection import train_test_split
from sklearn.metrics import precision_score, recall_score,
  accuracy_score

pipeline = Pipeline([
    ('vect', TfidfVectorizer(stop_words='english')),
    ('clf', LogisticRegression())
])
parameters = {
    'vect__max_df': (0.25, 0.5, 0.75),
    'vect__stop_words': ('english', None),
    'vect__max_features': (2500, 5000, 10000, None),
    'vect__ngram_range': ((1, 1), (1, 2)),
    'vect__use_idf': (True, False),
```

```
        'vect__norm': ('l1', 'l2'),
        'clf__penalty': ('l1', 'l2'),
        'clf__C': (0.01, 0.1, 1, 10),
}


df = pd.read_csv('./SMSSpamCollection', delimiter='t',
    header=None)
X = df[1].values
y = df[0].values
label_encoder = LabelEncoder()
y = label_encoder.fit_transform(y)
X_train, X_test, y_train, y_test = train_test_split(X, y)

grid_search = GridSearchCV(pipeline, parameters, n_jobs=-1,
    verbose=1, scoring='accuracy', cv=3)
grid_search.fit(X_train, y_train)
print('Best score: %0.3f' % grid_search.best_score_)
print('Best parameters set:')
best_parameters = grid_search.best_estimator_.get_params()
for param_name in sorted(parameters.keys()):
    print('t%s: %r' % (param_name, best_parameters[param_name]))
    predictions = grid_search.predict(X_test)
    print('Accuracy:', accuracy_score(y_test, predictions))
    print('Precision:', precision_score(y_test, predictions))
    print('Recall:', recall_score(y_test, predictions))


# Out[1]:
Fitting 3 folds for each of 576 candidates, totalling 1728
fits[Parallel(n_jobs=-1)]: Done   42 tasks       | elapsed:    4.5s
[Parallel(n_jobs=-1)]: Done 192 tasks       | elapsed:   23.5s
[Parallel(n_jobs=-1)]: Done 442 tasks       | elapsed:   57.2s
[Parallel(n_jobs=-1)]: Done 792 tasks       | elapsed: 1.8min
[Parallel(n_jobs=-1)]: Done 1242 tasks       | elapsed: 2.9min
[Parallel(n_jobs=-1)]: Done 1728 out of 1728 | elapsed:   6.0min finished
Best score: 0.983
Best parameters set:
   clf__C: 10
        clf__penalty: 'l2'
        vect__max_df: 0.25
        vect__max_features: 5000
  vect__ngram_range: (1, 2)
 vect__stop_words: None
    vect__use_idf: True
Accuracy: 0.983488872936
Precision: 0.99375
Recall: 0.878453038674
```

Optimizing the values of the hyperparameters has improved our model's recall score on the test set.

Multi-class classification

In previous sections, we learned to use logistic regression for binary classification. In many classification problems, however, there are more than two classes that are of interest. We might wish to predict the genres of songs from samples of audio, or to classify images of galaxies by their types. The goal of multi-class classification is to assign an instance to one of set of classes. scikit-learn uses a strategy called **one-versus-all**, or **one-versus-the-rest**, to support multi-class classification. One-versus-all classification uses one binary classifier for each of the possible classes. The class that is predicted with the greatest confidence is assigned to the instance. LogisticRegression supports multi-class classification using the one-versus-all strategy out of the box. Let's use LogisticRegression for a multi-class classification problem.

Assume that you would like to watch a movie, but you have a strong aversion to watching bad movies. To inform your decision, you could read reviews of the movies you are considering, but unfortunately you also have a strong aversion to reading movie reviews. Let's use scikit-learn to find the movies with good reviews.

In this example, we will classify the sentiments of phrases taken from movie reviews in the Rotten Tomatoes dataset. Each phrase can be classified as one of the following sentiments: negative, somewhat negative, neutral, somewhat positive, or positive. While the classes appear to be ordered, the explanatory variables that we will use do not always corroborate this order due to sarcasm, negation, and other linguistic phenomena. Instead, we will approach this problem as a multi-class classification task. The data can be downloaded from http://www.kaggle.com/c/sentiment-analysis-on-movie-reviews/data. First, let's explore the dataset using pandas. The columns of the dataset are tab-delimited. The dataset contains 156060 instances:

```
# In[1]:
import pandas as pd
df = pd.read_csv('./train.tsv', header=0, delimiter='t')
print(df.count())

# Out[1]:
PhraseId      156060
SentenceId    156060
Phrase        156060
Sentiment     156060
dtype: int64
```

```
# In[2]:
print(df.head())
```

```
# Out[2]:
   PhraseId  SentenceId                                              Phrase
0         1           1  A series of escapades demonstrating the adage ...
1         2           1  A series of escapades demonstrating the adage ...
2         3           1                                            A series
3         4           1                                                   A
4         5           1                                              series

   Sentiment
0          1
1          2
2          2
3          2
4          2
```

The `Sentiment` column contains the response variables. The label 0 corresponds to the sentiment negative, 1 corresponds to somewhat negative, and so on. The `Phrase` column contains the raw text. Each sentence from the movie reviews has been parsed into smaller phrases. We will not need the `PhraseId` and `SentenceId` columns in this example. Let's print some of the phrases and examine them:

```
# In[3]:
print(df['Phrase'].head(10))
```

```
# Out[3]:
0    A series of escapades demonstrating the adage ...
1    A series of escapades demonstrating the adage ...
2                                             A series
3                                                    A
4                                               series
5    of escapades demonstrating the adage that what...
6                                                   of
7    escapades demonstrating the adage that what is...
8                                            escapades
9    demonstrating the adage that what is good for ...
Name: Phrase, dtype: object
```

Now let's examine the target classes:

```
# In[4]:
print(df['Sentiment'].describe())
```

```
# Out[4]:
count    156060.000000
mean          2.063578
```

```
std            0.893832
min            0.000000
25%            2.000000
50%            2.000000
75%            3.000000
max            4.000000
Name: Sentiment, dtype: float64

# In[5]:
print(df['Sentiment'].value_counts())

# Out[5]:
2      79582
3      32927
1      27273
4       9206
0       7072
Name: Sentiment, dtype: int64

# In[6]:
print(df['Sentiment'].value_counts()/df['Sentiment'].count())

# Out[6]:
2      0.509945
3      0.210989
1      0.174760
4      0.058990
0      0.045316
Name: Sentiment, dtype: float64
```

The most common class, Neutral, includes more than *50%* of the instances. Accuracy will not be an informative performance measure for this problem, as a degenerate classifier that predicts only Neutral can obtain an accuracy near 0.5. Approximately one quarter of the reviews are positive or somewhat positive, and approximately one-fifth of the reviews are negative or somewhat negative. Let's train a classifier with scikit-learn:

```
# In[7]:
from sklearn.feature_extraction.text import TfidfVectorizer
from sklearn.linear_model.logistic import LogisticRegression
from sklearn.model_selection import train_test_split
from sklearn.metrics import classification_report, accuracy_score,
  confusion_matrix
from sklearn.pipeline import Pipeline
from sklearn.model_selection import GridSearchCV

df = pd.read_csv('./train.tsv', header=0, delimiter='t')
X, y = df['Phrase'], df['Sentiment'].as_matrix()
```

```
X_train, X_test, y_train, y_test = train_test_split(X, y,
   train_size=0.5)
grid_search = main(X_train, y_train)
pipeline = Pipeline([
    ('vect', TfidfVectorizer(stop_words='english')),
    ('clf', LogisticRegression())
])
parameters = {
    'vect__max_df': (0.25, 0.5),
     'vect__ngram_range': ((1, 1), (1, 2)),
     'vect__use_idf': (True, False),
     'clf__C': (0.1, 1, 10),
}
grid_search = GridSearchCV(pipeline, parameters, n_jobs=-1,
   verbose=1, scoring='accuracy')
grid_search.fit(X_train, y_train)
print('Best score: %0.3f' % grid_search.best_score_)
print('Best parameters set:')
best_parameters = grid_search.best_estimator_.get_params()
for param_name in sorted(parameters.keys()):
 print('t%s: %r' % (param_name, best_parameters[param_name]))

# Out[7]:
Fitting 3 folds for each of 24 candidates, totalling 72 fits
[Parallel(n_jobs=-1)]: Done   42 tasks       | elapsed:  1.6min
[Parallel(n_jobs=-1)]: Done   72 out of   72 | elapsed:  3.5min finished
Best score: 0.621
Best parameters set:
tclf__C: 10
tvect__max_df: 0.25
tvect__ngram_range: (1, 2)
tvect__use_idf: False
```

Multi-class classification performance metrics

As with binary classification, confusion matrices are useful for visualizing the types of errors made by the classifier. Precision, recall, and F1 score can also be computed for each of the classes and accuracy for all of the predictions can be calculated. Let's evaluate our classifier's predictions:

```
# In[8]:
predictions = grid_search.predict(X_test)
print('Accuracy: %s' % accuracy_score(y_test, predictions))
print('Confusion Matrix:')
print(confusion_matrix(y_test, predictions))
print('Classification Report:')
```

```
print(classification_report(y_test, predictions))

# Out[8]:
Accuracy: 0.636255286428
Confusion Matrix:
[[ 1124  1725   628    65    10]
 [  923  6049  6132   583    34]
 [  197  3131 32658  3640   137]
 [   15   398  6530  8234  1301]
 [    3    43   530  2358  1582]]
Classification Report:
             precision    recall  f1-score   support

          0       0.50      0.32      0.39      3552
          1       0.53      0.44      0.48     13721
          2       0.70      0.82      0.76     39763
          3       0.55      0.50      0.53     16478
          4       0.52      0.35      0.42      4516

avg / total       0.62      0.64      0.62     78030
```

First we make predictions using the best parameter set found from grid searching. While our classifier is an improvement over the baseline classifier, it frequently mistakes *Somewhat Positive* and *Somewhat Negative* for *Neutral*.

Multi-label classification and problem transformation

In previous sections, we discussed binary classification, in which each instance must be assigned to one of two classes, and multi-class classification, in which each instance must be assigned to one of a set of classes. The final type of classification problem that we will discuss is **multi-label classification**, in which each instance can be assigned a subset of the set of classes. Examples of multi-label classification include assigning tags to messages posted to a forum and classifying objects present in an image. There are two groups of approaches for multi-label classification.

Problem transformation methods are techniques that cast the original multi-label problem as a set of single-label classification problems. The first problem transformation method that we will review converts each set of labels encountered in the training data to a single label. For example, consider a multi-label classification problem in which news articles must be assigned to one or more categories from a set. The following training data contains seven articles that can pertain to one or more of five categories:

Instance	Local	US	Business	Science and Technology	Sports
1	✓	✓			
2	✓		✓		
3			✓	✓	
4					✓
5	✓				
6			✓		
7		✓		✓	

Transforming the problem into a single-label classification task using the power set of labels seen in the training data, results in the following training data. Previously, the first instance was classified as *Local* and *US*. Now it has a single label: *Local ∧ US*.

Instance	Local	Local ∧ US	Business	Local ∧ Business	US ∧ Science and Technology	Business ∧ Science and Technology	Sports
1		✓					
2				✓			
3						✓	
4							✓
5	✓						
6			✓				
7					✓		

The multi-label classification problem that had five classes is now a multi-class classification problem with seven classes. While the power set problem transformation is intuitive, increasing the number of classes is frequently impractical; this transformation can produce many new labels that correspond to only a few training instances. Furthermore, the classifier can only predict combinations of labels that were seen in the training data.

Instance	Local	¬Local		Instance	Business	¬Business
1	✓			1		✓
2	✓			2	✓	
3		✓		3	✓	
4		✓		4		✓
5	✓			5		✓
6		✓		6	✓	
7		✓		7		✓

Instance	Sci. and Tech.	¬Sci. and Tech.		Instance	Sports	¬Sports
1		✓		1		✓
2		✓		2		✓
3	✓			3		✓
4		✓		4	✓	
5		✓		5		✓
6		✓		6		✓
7	✓			7		✓

Instance	US	¬US
1	✓	
2	✓	
3		✓
4		✓
5		✓
6		✓
7	✓	

A second problem transformation strategy is to train one binary classifier for each of the labels in the training set. Each classifier predicts whether or not the instance belongs to one label. Our example would require five binary classifiers; the first classifier will predict whether or not an instance should be classified as *Local*, the second classifier will predict whether or not an instance should be classified as *US*, and so on. The final prediction is the union of the predictions from all of the binary classifiers. The transformed training data is shown in the previous figure. This problem transformation ensures that the single-label problems will have the same number of training examples as the multi-label problem, but ignores relationships between the labels.

Multi-label classification performance metrics

Multi-label classification problems must be assessed using different performance measures than single-label classification problems. Two of the most common performance metrics are **hamming loss** and **Jaccard similarity**. Hamming loss is the average fraction of incorrect labels. Note that hamming loss is a loss function and that the perfect score is *0*. Jaccard similarity, or the Jaccard index, is the size of the intersection of the predicted labels and the true labels divided by the size of the union of the predicted and true labels. It ranges from *0* to *1*, and 1 is the perfect score. Jaccard similarity is given by the following equation:

$$J(Predicted, True) = \frac{|Predicted \cap True|}{|Predicted \cup True|}$$

```
# In[1]:
import numpy as np
from sklearn.metrics import hamming_loss, jaccard_similarity_score

print(hamming_loss(np.array([[0.0, 1.0], [1.0, 1.0]]),
    np.array([[0.0, 1.0],
    [1.0, 1.0]])))

# Out[1]:
0.0

# In[2]:
print(hamming_loss(np.array([[0.0, 1.0], [1.0, 1.0]]),
    np.array([[1.0, 1.0],
    [1.0, 1.0]])))

# Out[2]:
0.25

# In[3]:
print(hamming_loss(np.array([[0.0, 1.0], [1.0, 1.0]]),
    np.array([[1.0, 1.0],
    [0.0, 1.0]])))

# Out[3]:
0.5

# In[4]:
print(jaccard_similarity_score(np.array([[0.0, 1.0], [1.0, 1.0]]),
    np.array([[0.0, 1.0], [1.0, 1.0]])))

# Out[4]:
1.0
```

```
# In[5]:
print(jaccard_similarity_score(np.array([[0.0, 1.0], [1.0, 1.0]]),
    np.array([[1.0, 1.0], [1.0, 1.0]])))

# Out[5]:
0.75

# In[6]:
print(jaccard_similarity_score(np.array([[0.0, 1.0], [1.0, 1.0]]),
    np.array([[1.0, 1.0], [0.0, 1.0]])))

# Out[6]:
0.5
```

Summary

In this chapter, we discussed generalized linear models; they extend ordinary linear regression to support response variables with non-normal distributions. Generalized linear models use a link function to relate a linear combination of the explanatory variables to the response variable; unlike ordinary linear regression, the modeled relationship does not need to be linear. In particular, we examined the logistic link function, a sigmoid function that returns a value between *0* and *1* for any real number.

We discussed logistic regression, a generalized linear model that uses the logistic link function to relate explanatory variables to a Bernoulli-distributed response variable. Logistic regression can be used for binary classification, a task in which an instance must be assigned to one of two classes. We used logistic regression to classify spam and ham SMS messages. We then discussed multi-class classification, a task in which each instance must be assigned one label from a set of labels. We used the one-versus-all strategy to classify the sentiments of movie reviews. Finally, we discussed multi-label classification, in which instances must be assigned a subset of a set of labels.

7
Naive Bayes

In previous chapters, we introduced two models for classification tasks: **k-Nearest Neighbors (KNN)** and logistic regression. In this chapter, we will introduce another family of classifiers called Naive Bayes. Named for its use of Bayes' theorem and for its naive assumption that all features are conditionally independent of each other given the response variable, Naive Bayes is the first generative model that we will discuss. First, we will introduce Bayes' theorem. Next, we will compare generative and discriminative models. We will discuss Naive Bayes and its assumptions and examine its common variants. Finally, we will fit a model using scikit-learn.

Bayes' theorem

Bayes' theorem is a formula for calculating the probability of an event using prior knowledge of related conditions. The theorem was discovered by an English statistician and minister named Thomas Bayes in the 18th century. Bayes never published his work; his notes were edited and published posthumously by the mathematician Richard Price. Bayes' theorem is given by the following formula:

$$P(A|B) = \frac{P(B|A)P(A)}{P(B)}$$

A and B are events; $P(A)$ is the probability of observing event A, and $P(B)$ is the probability of observing event B. $P(A|B)$ is the conditional probability of observing A given that B was observed. In classification tasks, our goal is to map features of explanatory variables to a discrete response variable; we must find the most likely label, A, given the features, B.

A theorem is a mathematical statement that has been proven to be true based on axioms or other theorems.

Let's work through an example. Assume that a patient exhibits a symptom of a particular disease, and that a doctor administers a test for that disease. This test has been found to have 99% recall and 98% specificity. **Specificity** measures the true negative rate, or the proportion of truly negative instances that were predicted to be negative. Specificity and recall are often used to evaluate medical tests; recall is sometimes called **sensitivity** in this context. Remember from previous chapters that 99% recall means that 99% of the patients who truly have the disease were predicted to have it. 98% specificity means that 98% of the patients who truly do not have the disease were predicted not to have it. Also assume that the disease is rare; the probability that a person in the population has it is only 0.2%. If the patient's test result is positive, what is the probability that she actually has the disease? More formally, what is the conditional probability of having the disease, *A*, given a positive test result, *B*?

We can this solve using Bayes' theorem if we know the values of the terms *P(A)*, *P(B)*, and *P(B|A)*. *P(A)* is the probability of having the disease, which we know to be 0.2%. *P(B|A)*, or the probability of a positive test result given that the patient has the disease, is the test's recall, 0.99. The last term we require is *P(B)*, the probability of a positive test result. This is equal to the sum of the probabilities of true and false positive results, as follows. Note that *not-Disease* is a single symbol, not a difference.

$$P(Positive) = P(Positive \mid Disease)P(Disease) + P(Positive \mid not - Disease)P(not - Disease)$$

The probability of a positive test result given that the patient has the disease is equal to the test's recall, 0.99. The probability of this outcome is the product of the test's recall and the probability of having the disease, 0.002. The probability of a positive test result given that the patient does not have the disease is the complement of the test's specificity, or 0.02. The probability of this outcome is the product of the complement of the test's specificity, 0.02, and the complement of the probability of having the disease, 0.998.

$$P(Positive) = 0.99 \times 0.002 + 0.02 \times 0.998 = 0.022$$

The following is Bayes' theorem re-written in terms of our events:

$$P(Disease \mid Positive) = \frac{P(Positive \mid Disease)P(Disease)}{P(Positive \mid Disease)P(Disease) + P(Positive \mid not-Disease)P(not-Disease)}$$

We have solved for all of the terms, and can now solve for the conditional probability of having the disease given a positive test result, as follows:

$$P(Disease \mid Positive) = \frac{0.99 \times 0.002}{0.99 \times 0.002 + 0.02 \times 0.998} = 0.09$$

The probability that a patient who tests positive truly has the disease is less than *10%*. This result may seem incorrect. The test's recall and specificity were *99%* and *98%*, respectively; it is not intuitive that a patient who tests positive is much more likely not to have the disease. While the test's specificity and recall are similar, false positives are much more frequent than false negatives because the probability of having the disease is very small. In a population of *1,000* patients, we expect only 2 to have the disease. With *99%* recall, we should expect the test to correctly detect these two patients. However, we should also expect the test to incorrectly predict that almost 20 other patients have the disease. Only *9%* of the *22* positive predictions are true positives.

Generative and discriminative models

In classification tasks, our goal is to learn the parameters of a model that optimally maps features of the explanatory variables to the response variable. All of the classifiers that we have previously discussed are **discriminative models**, which learn a decision boundary that is used to discriminate between classes. Probabilistic discriminative models, such as logistic regression, learn to estimate the conditional probability $P(y \mid x)$; they learn to estimate which class is most likely given the input features. Non-probabilistic discriminative models, such as KNN, directly map features to classes.

Generative models do not directly learn a decision boundary. Instead, they model the joint probability distribution of the features and the classes, $P(x, y)$. This is equivalent to modelling the probabilities of the classes and the probabilities of the features given the classes. That is, generative models model how the classes generate features. Bayes' theorem can then be applied to a generative model to estimate the conditional probability of a class given the features.

If our goal in classification tasks is to map features to classes, why would we use an approach that requires an intermediate step? Why choose a generative model instead of a discriminative model? One reason is that generative models can be used to generate new examples of the data. More importantly, generative models can be more biased than their discriminative counterparts because they model how the classes generate data. This intermediate step introduces more assumptions to the model. When these assumptions hold, generative models are more robust to noisy training data and may perform better than discriminative models when training data is scarce. The disadvantage is that these assumptions can prevent generative models from learning; discriminative models generally perform better than generative models as the number of training instances increases.

Naive Bayes

In the first section of this chapter, we described Bayes' theorem. Recall that it is given by the following:

$$P(A \mid B) = \frac{P(B \mid A) P(A)}{P(B)}$$

Let's rewrite Bayes' theorem in terms that are more natural for a classification task:

$$P(y \mid x_1, \ldots, x_n) = \frac{P(x_1, \ldots, x_n \mid y) P(y)}{P(x_1, \ldots, x_n)}$$

In the preceding formula, y is the positive class, x_1 is the first feature for the instance, and n is the number of features. $P(B)$ is constant for all inputs, so we can omit it; the probability of observing a particular feature in the training set does not vary for different test instances. This leaves two terms: the prior class probability, $P(y)$, and the conditional probability, $P(x_1, \ldots, x_{n|y})$. Naive Bayes estimates these terms using maximum a posteriori estimation. $P(y)$ is simply the frequency of each class in the training set. For categorical features, $P(x_i|y)$ is simply the frequency of the feature in the training instances belonging to that class. Its estimate is given by the following formula:

$$\hat{P}(x_i \mid y_i) = \frac{N_{x_i, y_j}}{N_{y_j}}$$

The numerator is the number of times that the feature appears in training samples of class y_j. The denominator is the total frequency of all features for class y_j. Naive Bayes predicts the class with the greatest probability, as given by this formula:

$$\hat{y} = \text{argmax}_y P(y) \prod_{i=1}^{n} P(x_i \mid y)$$

Note that even when a Naive Bayes classifier performs well, the estimated class probabilities can be poorly calibrated. The variants of Naive Bayes differ mostly in their assumptions about the distribution of $P(x_i|y)$, and therefore the types of features that they can learn from. The variant we have discussed, **multinomial Naive Bayes**, is suitable for categorical features. Our term frequency features represent each token in a corpus as a categorical variable. **Gaussian Naive Bayes** is suitable for continuous features; it assumes that each feature is normally distributed for each class. **Bernoulli Naive Bayes** is suitable when all of the features are binary-valued. scikit-learn's `GaussianNB`, `BernoulliNB`, and `MultinomialNB` classes implement these variants.

Assumptions of Naive Bayes

The model is called **Naive** because it assumes that the features are conditionally independent given the response variable:

$$P(x_i \mid y) = P(x_i \mid y, x_j)$$

Note that this is not equivalent to assuming that the features are independent, as given by the following:

$$P(x_i) = P(x_i \mid x_j)$$

This independence assumption is seldom true. However, Naive Bayes can effectively discriminate between linearly separable classes even when this assumption is violated, and often performs better than discriminative models when training data is scarce. In addition to performing well, Naive Bayes models are typically fast and simple to implement; it is widely used for these reasons.

Consider an article classification task for a news site. Given an article, our goal is to assign it to a newspaper section, such as "International Politics", "U.S. Politics", "Science and Technology" or "Sports". The Naive Bayes assumption means that knowing that an article belongs to the sports section and knowing that the article contains the word "basketball" does not affect your beliefs about whether the words "Warriors" or "UNC" appear in the article. This assumption does not hold in this task; knowing that an article is from the "Sports" section and that it contains the word "basketball" should make us believe that it is more likely to contain the words "UNC", "*NCAA*", and "Michael Jordan", and less likely to contain unrelated words such as "sandwich" or "meteor". Knowing that an article belongs to the sports section and contains the word "Duke" should make us more believe that it is more likely to contain the words "trip" and "flop". While the Naive Bayes assumption seldom holds, it is necessary; the model would have an impractical number of parameters without it, and it allows class conditional probabilities to be estimated directly from the training data.

Naive Bayes also assumes that training instances are **independent and identically distributed (i.i.d)**, this means that training instances are independent from each other and are drawn from the same probability distribution. Repeatedly tossing a coin produces i.i.d. samples; the probability of each flip landing heads is the same, and the outcome of any flip does not depend on the outcome of any other flip. Unlike the conditional independence assumption, this assumption must hold for Naive Bayes to perform well.

Naive Bayes with scikit-learn

Let's fit a Naive Bayes classifier with scikit-learn. We will compare the performances of Naive Bayes and logistic regression classifiers on increasingly large samples of two different training sets. The Breast Cancer Wisconsin dataset consists of features extracted from fine needle aspirate images of breast masses. The task is to classify masses as malignant or benign using 30 real-valued features that describe the cell nuclei in each fine needle aspirate image. The dataset has 212 malignant instances and 357 benign instances. The Pima Indians Diabetes Database task is to predict whether an individual has diabetes using eight features representing the number of times the individual has been pregnant, measures from an oral glucose tolerance test, diastolic blood pressure, triceps skin fold thickness, body mass index, age, and other diagnostics. The dataset has 268 diabetic instances and 500 non-diabetic instances:

```
# In[1]:
%matplotlib inline

# In[2]:
import pandas as pd
```

```python
from sklearn.datasets import load_breast_cancer
from sklearn.linear_model import LogisticRegression
from sklearn.naive_bayes import GaussianNB
from sklearn.model_selection import train_test_split
import matplotlib.pyplot as plt

X, y = load_breast_cancer(return_X_y=True)
X_train, X_test, y_train, y_test = train_test_split(X, y, stratify=y,
  test_size=0.2, random_state=31)

lr = LogisticRegression()
nb = GaussianNB()

lr_scores = []
nb_scores = []

train_sizes = range(10, len(X_train), 25)

for train_size in train_sizes:
    X_slice, _, y_slice, _ = train_test_split(
    X_train, y_train, train_size=train_size, stratify=y_train,
random_state=31)
    nb.fit(X_slice, y_slice)
    nb_scores.append(nb.score(X_test, y_test))
    lr.fit(X_slice, y_slice)
    lr_scores.append(lr.score(X_test, y_test))

plt.plot(train_sizes, nb_scores, label='Naïve Bayes')
plt.plot(train_sizes, lr_scores, linestyle='--', label='Logistic
Regression')
plt.title("Naïve Bayes and Logistic Regression Accuracies")
plt.xlabel("Number of training instances")
plt.ylabel("Test set accuracy")
plt.legend()

# Out[2]:
<matplotlib.legend.Legend at 0x7ff86c658668>
```

Let's start with the Breast Cancer Wisconsin dataset. The magic command `%matplotlib inline` allows plots to be displayed directly in the notebook. We load the dataset using scikit-learn's `load_breast_cancer` convenience function. Then we split off *20%* of the instances to use as a test set using the `train_test_split` convenience function. `stratify=y` specifies that the training and test sets should have equal proportions of positive and negative instances; this is important when the classes are imbalanced, as sampling instances uniformly at random could result in a training or testing set with few instances of the minority class. We will evaluate all of the models using this testing set. We use `train_test_split` again to take increasingly large slices of the remaining instances, and use them to train `LogisticRegression` and `GaussianNB` classifiers. Finally, we plot the classifiers' scores.

Naive Bayes classifiers often outperform logistic regression classifiers on small datasets; Naive Bayes is more biased, which prevents it from overfitting noise. However, this bias also can also stunt the model's learning on large datasets. In this example, the Naive Bayes classifier initially performs better than the logistic regression classifier, but the logistic regression classifier's performance improves as the size of the training set increases.

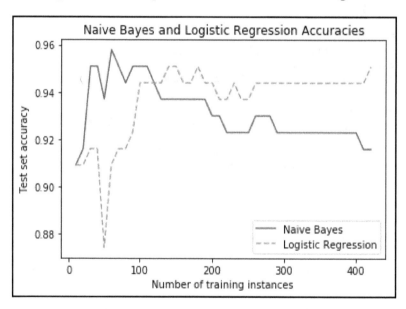

Now let's compare the performances of logistic regression and Naïve Bayes classifiers on the Pima Indians Diabetes Database:

```
# In[3]:
df = pd.read_csv('./pima-indians-diabetes.data', header=None)
y = df[8]
X = df[[0, 1, 2, 3, 4, 5, 6, 7]]
X_train, X_test, y_train, y_test = train_test_split(X, y, stratify=y,
    random_state=11)

lr = LogisticRegression()
nb = GaussianNB()
lr_scores = []
nb_scores = []

train_sizes = range(10, len(X_train), 10)
for train_size in train_sizes:
    X_slice, _, y_slice, _ = train_test_split(
        X_train, y_train, train_size=train_size, stratify=y_train,
            random_state=11)
    nb.fit(X_slice, y_slice)
    nb_scores.append(nb.score(X_test, y_test))
    lr.fit(X_slice, y_slice)
    lr_scores.append(lr.score(X_test, y_test))

plt.plot(train_sizes, nb_scores, label='Naïve Bayes')
plt.plot(train_sizes, lr_scores, linestyle='--', label='Logistic
Regression')
plt.title("Naïve Bayes and Logistic Regression Accuracies")
plt.xlabel("Number of training instances")
plt.ylabel("Test set accuracy")
plt.legend()

# Out[3]:
<matplotlib.legend.Legend at 0x7ff86cb3eda0>
```

First, we use pandas to load the .csv file. The .csv file lacks a header row, so we split the response variable from the features using the column indices. Next, we create a stratified test set. Again, we train and evaluate models on increasingly large samples of the training set, and plot the accuracies. The Naive Bayes classifier is more accurate than the logistic regression classifier on small datasets, but the accuracy of the logistic regression classifier continues to improve as the size of the dataset increases.

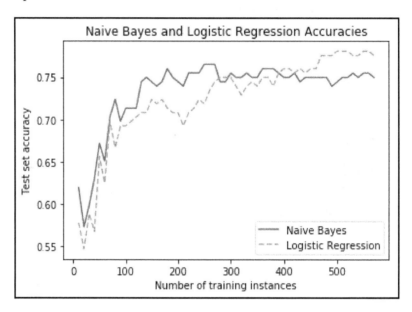

Summary

In this chapter, we introduced our first generative model, Naive Bayes. We used Bayes' theorem to calculate the probability that a patient who tests positive for a disease actually has the disease, using our knowledge of the test's performance and related conditions. We compared generative and discriminative models, used scikit-learn to train a Naive Bayes classifier, and compared its performance with that of a discriminative model.

8
Nonlinear Classification and Regression with Decision Trees

In this chapter, we will discuss a simple, nonlinear model for classification and regression tasks called the **decision tree**. We'll use decision trees to build an ad blocker that can learn to classify images on a web page as banner advertisements or page content. While decision trees are seldom used in practice, they are components of more powerful models; understanding decision trees is important for this reason.

Decision trees

Decision trees are tree-like graphs that model a decision. They are analogous to the parlor game *Twenty Questions*. In *Twenty Questions*, one player, called the **answerer**, chooses an object but does not reveal the object to the other players, who are called **questioners**. The object should be a common noun, such as "guitar" or "sandwich", but not "1969 Gibson Les Paul Custom" or "North Carolina". The questioners must guess the object by asking as many as twenty questions that can be answered with "yes", "no", or "maybe". An intuitive strategy for questioners is to ask questions of increasing specificity; asking "is it a musical instrument?" as the first question will not efficiently reduce the number of possibilities, on average. The branches of a decision tree specify the shortest sequences of features that can be examined in order to estimate the value of a response variable. To continue the analogy, in *Twenty Questions*, the questioner and the answerer all have knowledge of the training data, but only the answerer knows the values of the features for the test instance. Decision trees are commonly learned by recursively splitting the set of training instances into subsets based on instances' features.

The following diagram depicts a decision tree that we will learn later in the chapter:

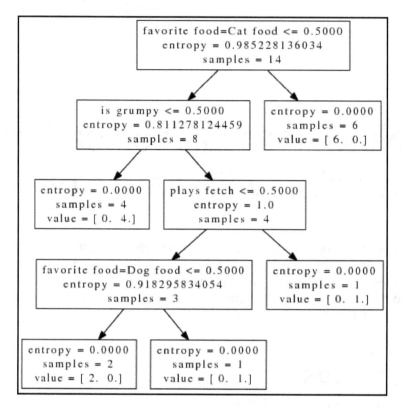

Represented by boxes, the interior nodes of the decision tree test features. These nodes are connected by edges that specify the possible outcomes of the tests. The training instances are divided into subsets based on the outcomes of the tests. For example, a node might test whether or not the value of a feature exceeds a threshold. The instances that pass the test will follow an edge to the node's right child, and the instances that fail the test will follow an edge to the node's left child. The children nodes similarly test their subsets of the training instances until a stopping criterion is satisfied. In classification tasks, the leaf nodes of the decision tree represent classes. In regression tasks, the values of the response variable for the instances contained in a leaf node may be averaged to produce the estimate for the response variable. After the decision tree has been constructed, making a prediction for a test instance requires only following the edges until a leaf node is reached.

Training decision trees

Let's create a decision tree using an algorithm called **Iterative Dichotomiser 3 (ID3)**. Invented by Ross Quinlan, ID3 was one of the first algorithms used to train decision trees. Assume that you are tasked with classifying animals as cats or dogs. Unfortunately, you cannot observe the animals directly and must use only a few attributes of the animals to make your decision. For each animal, you are told whether or not it likes to play fetch, whether or not it is frequently grumpy, and its favorite of three types of food. To classify new animals, the decision tree will examine a feature at each node. The edge it follows to the next node will depend on the outcome of the test. For example, the first node might ask whether or not the animal likes to play fetch. If the animal does, we will follow the edge to the left child node; if not, we will follow the edge to the right child node. Eventually an edge will connect to a leaf node that indicates whether the animal is a cat or a dog. The following fourteen instances comprise our training data:

Training instance	Plays fetch	Is grumpy	Favorite food	species
1	Yes	No	Bacon	Dog
2	No	Yes	Dog food	Dog
3	No	Yes	Cat food	Cat
4	No	Yes	Bacon	Cat
5	No	No	Cat food	Cat
6	No	Yes	Bacon	Cat
7	No	Yes	Cat food	Cat
8	No	No	Dog food	Dog
9	No	Yes	Cat food	Cat
10	Yes	No	Dog food	Dog
11	Yes	No	Bacon	Dog
12	No	No	Cat food	Cat
13	Yes	Yes	Cat food	Cat
14	Yes	Yes	Bacon	Dog

From this data, we can see that cats are generally grumpier than the dogs. Most dogs play fetch, and most cats refuse. Dogs prefer dog food and bacon, whereas cats only like cat food and bacon. The *is grumpy* and *plays fetch* explanatory variables can be easily converted to binary-valued features. The *favorite food* explanatory variable is a categorical variable that has three possible values; we will one-hot encode it. Recall that one-hot encoding represents a categorical variable with as many binary-valued features as there are values for variable. Since *favorite food* has three possible states, we will represent it with three binary-valued features. From this table, we can manually construct classification rules. For example, an animal that is grumpy and likes cat food must be a cat, while an animal that plays fetch and likes bacon must be a dog. Constructing these classification rules by hand for even a small dataset is cumbersome. Instead, we will learn these rules using ID3.

Selecting the questions

Like *Twenty Questions*, the decision tree will estimate the value of the response variable by testing the values of a sequence of features. Which feature should be tested first? Intuitively, a test that produces subsets that contain all cats or all dogs is better than a test that produces subsets that contain both cats and dogs. If the members of a subset are of different classes, we are still uncertain about how to classify the instance. We should also avoid creating tests that separate only a single cat or dog from the others; such tests are analogous to asking specific questions in the first few rounds of *Twenty Questions*. These tests can infrequently classify an instance and will not likely reduce our uncertainty. The tests that reduce our uncertainty about the classification the most are the best. We can quantify the amount of uncertainty using a measure called **entropy**. Measured in bits, entropy quantifies the amount of uncertainty in a variable. Entropy is given by the following equation, where n is the number of outcomes and $P(x_i)$ is the probability of outcome i. Common values for b are 2, e, and 10. Because the log of a number less than 1 will be negative, the entire sum is negated to return a positive value.

$$H(X) = -\sum_{i=1}^{n} P(x_i) \log_b P(x_i)$$

For example, a single toss of a fair coin has only two outcomes: heads and tails. The probability that the coin will land on heads is *0.5*, and the probability that it will land on tails is *0.5*. The entropy of the coin toss is equal to the following:

$$H(X) = -(0.5 \log_2 0.5 + 0.5 \log_2 0.5) = 1.0$$

That is, only *1* bit is required to represent the two equally probable outcomes, heads and tails. Two tosses of a fair coin can result in four possible outcomes: heads and heads, heads and tails, tails and heads, and tails and tails. The probability of each outcome is *0.25*. The entropy of two tosses is equal to the following:

$$H(X) = -(0.25 \log_2 0.25 + 0.25 \log_2 0.25 + 0.25 \log_2 0.25 + 0.25 \log_2 0.25) = 2.0$$

If the coin has the same face on both sides, the variable representing its outcome has zero bits of entropy; that is, we are always certain of the outcome and the variable will never represent new information. Entropy can also be represented as a fraction of a bit. For example, an unfair coin has two different faces but is weighted such that the faces are not equally likely to land in a toss. Assume that the probability that an unfair coin will land on heads is *0.8*, and the probability that it will land on tails is *0.2*. The entropy of a single toss of this coin is equal to this:

$$H(X) = -(0.8 \log_2 0.8 + 0.2 \log_2 0.2) = 0.72$$

The outcome of a single toss of an unfair coin can have a fraction of *1* bit of entropy. There are two possible outcomes of the toss, but we are not totally uncertain since one outcome is more frequent.

Let's calculate the entropy of classifying an unknown animal. If an equal number of dogs and cats comprise our animal classification training data and we do not know anything else about the animal, the entropy of the decision is equal to *1*. All we know is that the animal could be either a cat or a dog; like the fair coin toss, both outcomes are equally likely. Our training data, however, contains six dogs and eight cats. If we do not know anything else about the unknown animal, the entropy of the decision is given by the following:

$$H(X) = -\left(\frac{6}{14} \log_2 \frac{6}{14} + \frac{8}{14} \log_2 \frac{8}{14}\right) = 0.99$$

Since cats are more common, we are slightly less uncertain about the outcome. Now let's find the feature that will be most helpful in classifying the animal; that is, let's find the feature that reduces the entropy the most. We can test the **plays fetch** feature, and divide the training instances into animals that play fetch and animals that don't. This produces the following two subsets:

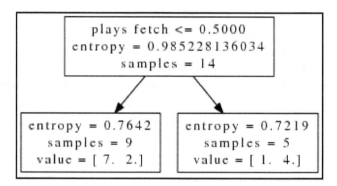

Decision trees are often visualized as diagrams that are similar to flowcharts. The top box of the previous diagram is the root node; it contains all of our training instances and specifies the feature that will be tested. At the root node, we have not eliminated any instances from the training set, and the **entropy** is equal to approximately **0.99**. The root node tests the **plays fetch** feature. Recall that we converted the this Boolean explanatory variable to a binary-valued feature. Training instances for which **plays fetch** is equal to zero follow the edge to the root's left child, and training instances for animals that do play fetch follow the edge to the root's right child node. The left child node contains a subset of the training data with seven cats and two dogs that do not like to play fetch. The entropy at this node is given by the following:

$$H(X) = -(\tfrac{2}{9} \log_2 \tfrac{2}{9} + \tfrac{7}{9} \log_2 \tfrac{7}{9}) = 0.76$$

The right child contains a subset with one cat and four dogs that do like to play fetch. The entropy at this node is given by:

$$H(X) = -\left(\frac{1}{5} \log_2 \frac{1}{5} + \frac{4}{5} \log_2 \frac{4}{5} \right) = 0.72$$

Instead of testing the **plays fetch** feature, we could test the **is grumpy** feature. This test produces the following tree. As with the previous tree, instances that fail the test follow the left edge and instances that pass the test follow the right edge.

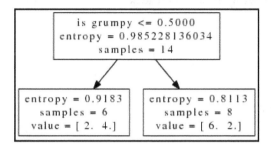

We could also divide the instances into animals that prefer cat food and animals that don't to produce the following tree:

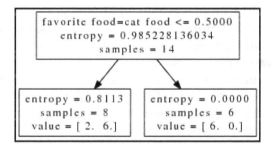

Information gain

Testing for the animals that prefer cat food resulted in one subset with six cats, zero dogs, and zero bits of entropy, and another subset with two cats, six dogs, and *0.811* bits of entropy. How can we measure which of these tests reduced our uncertainty about the classification the most? Averaging the entropies of the subsets may seem to be an appropriate measure of the reduction in entropy. In this example, the subsets produced by the cat food test have the lowest average entropy. Intuitively, this test seems to be effective, as we can use it to classify almost half of the training instances.

However, selecting the test that produces the subsets with the lowest average entropy can produce a sub-optimal tree. For example, imagine a test that produced one subset with two dogs and no cats, and another subset with four dogs and eight cats. The entropy of the first subset is equal to the following. Note that the second term is omitted because it is undefined:

$$H(X) = -\left(\frac{2}{2} \log_2 \frac{2}{2} \right) = 0.0$$

The entropy of the second subset is equal to:

$$H(X) = -\left(\frac{4}{12} \log_2 \frac{4}{12} + \frac{8}{12} \log_2 \frac{8}{12} \right) = 0.92$$

The average of these subsets' entropies is only *0.459*, but the subset containing most of the instances has almost one bit of entropy. This is analogous to asking specific questions early in *Twenty Questions*; we could get lucky and win within the first few attempts, but it is more likely that we will squander our questions without eliminating many possibilities. Instead, we will measure the reduction in entropy using a metric called **information gain**. Calculated with the following equation, information gain is the difference between the entropy of the parent node, *H(T)*, and the weighted average of the children nodes' entropies. *T* is the set of instances, and *a* is the feature under test.

$$IG(T, a) = H(T) - \sum_{v \in vals(a)} \frac{|\{x \in T | x_a = v\}|}{|T|} H(\{x \in T | x_a = v\})$$

The $X_a \in vals(a)$ is the value of attribute a for instance x. $\{X \in T \mid X_a = v\}$ is the number of instances for which attribute a is equal to value v. $H(\{X \in T \mid X_a = v\})$ is the entropy of the subset of instances for which the value of feature a is v. The following table contains the information gains for all of the tests. In this case, the cat food test is still the best, as it increases the information gain the most.

Test	Parent's entropy	First Child's entropy	Second Child's entropy	Weighted average	IG
plays fetch?	0.9852	0.7642	0.7219	0.7490 * 9/14 + 0.7219 * 5/14 = 0.7491	0.2361
is grumpy?	0.9852	0.9183	0.8113	0.9183 * 6/14 + 0.8113 * 8/14 = 0.85710.8572	0.1280
favorite food=cat food	0.9852	0.8113	0	0.8113 * 8 /14 + 0.0 * 6/14 = 0.4636	0.5216
favorite food=dog food	0.9852	0.8454	0	0.8454 * 11/14 + 0.0 * 3/14 = 0.6642	0.3210
favorite food=bacon	0.9852	0.9183	0.971	0.9183 * 9/14 + 0.9710 * 5/14 = 0.9371	0.0481

Now let's add another node to the tree. One of the child nodes produced by the test is a leaf node that contains only cats. The other node still contains two cats and six dogs. We will add a test to this node. Which of the remaining features reduces our uncertainty the most? The following table contains the information gains for all of the possible tests.

Test	Parent's entropy	First Child's entropy	Second Child's entropy	Weighted average	IG
plays fetch?	0.8113	1	0	1.0 * 4/8 + 0 * 4/8 = 0.5	0.3113
is grumpy?	0.8113	0	1	0.0 * 4/8 + 1 * 4/8 = 0.5	0.3113
favorite food=dog food	0.8113	0.9710	0	0.9710 * 5/8 + 0.0 * 3/8 = 0.6069	0.2044
favorite food=bacon	0.8113	0	0.9710	0.0 * 3/8 + 0.9710 * 5/8 = 0.6069	0.2044

All of the tests produce subsets with 0 bits of entropy, but the **is grumpy** and **plays fetch** tests produce the greatest information gain. ID3 breaks ties by selecting one of the best tests arbitrarily. We will select the **is grumpy** test, which splits its parent's eight instances into a leaf node containing four dogs, and a node containing two cats and two dogs. The following is a diagram of the current tree:

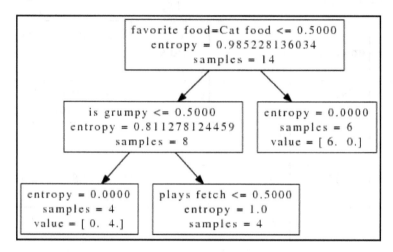

We will now select another explanatory variable to test the child node's four instances. The remaining tests, **favorite food=bacon**, **favorite food=dog food**, and **plays fetch**, all produce a leaf node containing one dog or cat and a node containing the remaining animals. That is, the remaining tests produce equal information gains, as shown in the following table:

Test	Parent's entropy	First Child's entropy	Second Child's entropy	Weighted average	Information gain
plays fetch?	1	0.9183	0	0.688725	0.311275
favorite food=dog food	1	0.9183	0	0.688725	0.311275
favorite food=bacon	1	0	0.9183	0.688725	0.311275

We will arbitrarily select the **plays fetch** test to produce a leaf node containing one dog and a node containing two cats and a dog. Two features remain: we can test for animals that like bacon, or we can test for animals that like dog food. Both of the tests will produce the same subsets, and create a leaf node containing one dog and a leaf node containing two cats. We will arbitrarily choose to test for animals that like dog food. Here is a diagram of the completed decision tree:

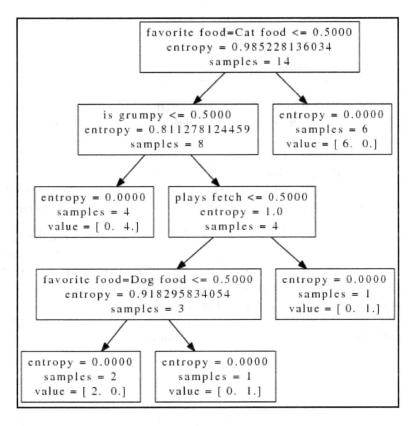

Let's classify some animals from the following test data:

Testing instance	Plays fetch	Is grumpy	Favorite food	Species
1	Yes	No	Bacon	Dog
2	Yes	Yes	Dog food	Dog
3	No	Yes	Dog food	Cat
4	No	Yes	Bacon	Cat
5	No	No	Cat food	Cat

Let's classify the first animal, which likes to plays fetch, is infrequently grumpy, and loves bacon. We will follow the edge to the root node's left child since the animal's favorite food is not cat food. The animal is not grumpy, so we will follow the edge to the second-level node's left child. This is a leaf node containing only dogs; we have correctly classified this instance. To classify the third test instance as a cat, we follow the edge to the root node's left child, follow the edge to the second-level node's right child, follow the edge to the third-level node's left child, and finally follow the edge to the fourth-level node's right child.

ID3 is not the only algorithm can be used to train decision trees. **C4.5** is a modified version of ID3 that can be used with continuous explanatory variables and can accommodate missing values for features. C4.5 can also **prune** trees. Pruning reduces the size of a tree by replacing branches that classify few instances with leaf nodes. Used by scikit-learn's implementation of decision trees, **CART** is another learning algorithm that supports pruning. Now that we have an understanding of the ID3 algorithm and an appreciation for the labor it automates, we will discuss building decision tress with scikit-learn.

Gini impurity

In the previous section, we built a decision tree by creating nodes that produced the greatest information gain. Another common heuristic for learning decision trees is **Gini impurity**, which measures the proportions of classes in a set. Gini impurity is given by the following equation, where j is the number of classes, t is the subset of instances for the node, and $P(i|t)$ is the probability of selecting an element of class i from the node's subset:

$$Gini(t) = 1 - \sum_{i=1}^{j} P(i|t)^2$$

Intuitively, Gini impurity is *0* when all the elements of the set are the same class, as the probability of selecting an element of that class is equal to *1*. Like entropy, Gini impurity is greatest when each class has an equal probability of being selected. The maximum value of Gini impurity depends on the number of possible classes and is given by the following equation:

$$Gini_{max} = 1 - \frac{1}{n}$$

Our problem has two classes, so the maximum value of the Gini impurity measure will be equal to *1/2*. scikit-learn supports learning decision trees using both information gain and Gini impurity. There are no firm rules for deciding when to use one criterion or the other; in practice, they often produce similar results. As with many decisions in machine learning, it is best to compare the performances of models trained using both options.

Decision trees with scikit-learn

Let's use decision trees to create software that can block banner ads on web pages. This program will predict whether each of the images on a web page is an advertisement or article content. Images that are classified as being advertisements could then be removed from the page. We will train a decision tree classifier using the Internet Advertisements dataset from `http://archive.ics.uci.edu/ml/datasets/Internet+Advertisements`, which contains data for *3,279* images. The proportions of the classes are imbalanced; *459* of the images are advertisements and *2,820* are content. Decision tree learning algorithms can produced biased trees from data with unbalanced class proportions; we will evaluate a model on the unaltered dataset before deciding whether it is worth balancing the training data by over- or under-sampling instances. The explanatory variables are the dimensions of the image, words from the containing page's URL, words from the image's URL, the image's alt text, the image's anchor text, and a window of words surrounding the image tag. The response variable is the image's class. The explanatory variables have already been transformed into features. The first three features are real numbers that encode the width, height, and aspect ratio of the images. The remaining features encode binary term frequencies for the text variables. In the following sample, we will grid-search for the hyperparameter values that produce the decision tree with the greatest accuracy, and then evaluate the tree's performance on a test set:

```
# In[1]:
import pandas as pd
from sklearn.tree import DecisionTreeClassifier
from sklearn.model_selection import train_test_split
from sklearn.metrics import classification_report
```

```
from sklearn.pipeline import Pipeline
from sklearn.grid_search import GridSearchCV

df = pd.read_csv('./ad.data', header=None)

explanatory_variable_columns = set(df.columns.values)
explanatory_variable_columns.remove(len(df.columns.values)-1)
response_variable_column = df[len(df.columns.values)-1] # The last column
describes the classes

y = [1 if e == 'ad.' else 0 for e in response_variable_column]
X = df[list(explanatory_variable_columns)].copy()
X.replace(to_replace=' *?', value=-1, regex=True, inplace=True)
X_train, X_test, y_train, y_test = train_test_split(X, y)

pipeline = Pipeline([
    ('clf', DecisionTreeClassifier(criterion='entropy'))
])
parameters = {
    'clf__max_depth': (150, 155, 160),
    'clf__min_samples_split': (2, 3),
    'clf__min_samples_leaf': (1, 2, 3)
}

grid_search = GridSearchCV(pipeline, parameters, n_jobs=-1, verbose=1,
    scoring='f1')
grid_search.fit(X_train, y_train)

best_parameters = grid_search.best_estimator_.get_params()
print('Best score: %0.3f' % grid_search.best_score_)
print('Best parameters set:')
for param_name in sorted(parameters.keys()):
    print('t%s: %r' % (param_name, best_parameters[param_name]))

predictions = grid_search.predict(X_test)
print(classification_report(y_test, predictions))

# Out[1]:
Fitting 3 folds for each of 18 candidates, totalling 54 fits
[Parallel(n_jobs=-1)]: Done   42 tasks       | elapsed:    5.4s
[Parallel(n_jobs=-1)]: Done   54 out of   54 | elapsed:    6.6s finished
Best score: 0.887
Best parameters set:
tclf__max_depth: 150
tclf__min_samples_leaf: 1
tclf__min_samples_split: 3
            precision    recall  f1-score   support
        0       0.98      0.99      0.98       717
```

1	0.92	0.83	0.87	103
avg / total	0.97	0.97	0.97	820

First we read the `.csv` using pandas. The `.csv` does not have a header row, so we split the last column containing the response variable's values from the features using its index. We encoded the advertisements as the positive class and the content as the negative class. More than one quarter of the instances are missing at least one of the values for the image's dimensions. These missing values are marked by whitespace and a question mark. We replaced the missing values with negative one, but we could have imputed the missing values; for instance, we could have replaced the missing height values with the average height value. We then split the data into training and test sets. We created a pipeline and an instance of `DecisionTreeClassifier`. We set the `criterion` keyword argument to `entropy` to build the tree using the information gain heuristic. Next, we specified the hyperparameter space for the grid search. We set `GridSearchCV` to maximize the model's F1 score. The classifier detected more than *80%* of the ads in the test set, and approximately *92%* of the images it predicted were ads were truly ads. Overall, the performance is promising; in later sections, we will try to modify our model to improve its performance.

Advantages and disadvantages of decision trees

The compromises associated with using decision trees are different from those of the other models we have discussed. Decision trees are easy to use. Unlike many learning algorithms, decision trees do not require the data to be standardized. While decision trees can tolerate missing values for features, scikit-learn's current implementation cannot. Decision trees can learn to ignore features that are not relevant to the task, and can be used to determine which features are most useful. Decision trees support multi-output tasks, and a single decision tree can be used for multi-class classification without employing a strategy like one versus all. Small decision trees can be easy to interpret and visualize with the `export_graphviz` function from scikit-learn's `tree` module.

Like most of the other models we have discussed, decision trees are **eager learners**. Eager learners must build an input-independent model from the training data before they can be used to estimate the values of test instances, but can predict relatively quickly once the model has been built. In contrast, **lazy learners** such as the KNN algorithm defer all generalization until they must make a prediction. Lazy learners do not spend time training, but often predict slowly compared to eager learners.

Decision trees are more prone to overfitting than many of the models we have discussed, as their learning algorithms can produce large, complicated decision trees that perfectly model every training instance but fail to generalize the real relationship. Several techniques can mitigate overfitting in decision trees. Pruning is a common strategy that removes some of the tallest nodes and leaves of a decision tree, but it is not currently implemented in scikit-learn. However, similar effects can be achieved through pre-pruning by setting a maximum depth for the tree, or by creating child nodes only when the number of training instances they will contain exceeds a threshold. The `DecisionTreeClassifier` and `DecisionTreeRegressor` classes provide keyword arguments for setting these constraints. Another technique for reducing overfitting is creating multiple decision trees from subsets of the training data and features. This collection of models is called an **ensemble**. In the next chapter, we will create an ensemble of decision trees called a **random forest**.

Efficient decision tree learning algorithms like ID3 are greedy. They learn efficiently by making locally optimal decisions, but are not guaranteed to produce the globally optimal tree. ID3 constructs a tree by selecting a sequence of features to test. Each feature is selected because it reduces the uncertainty in the node more than the other variables. It is possible, however, that locally sub-optimal tests are required in order to find the globally optimal tree. In our toy examples, the size of the tree did not matter since we retained all of nodes. In a real application, however, the tree's growth could be limited by pruning or similar mechanisms. Pruning trees with different shapes can produce trees with different performances. In practice, locally optimal decisions that are guided by the information gain or Gini impurity heuristics often result in acceptable decision trees.

Summary

In this chapter, we learned about simple non-linear models for classification and regression called decision trees. Like the parlor game *Twenty Questions*, decision trees are composed of sequences of questions that examine a test instance. The branches of a decision tree terminate in leaves that specify the predicted value of the response variable. We discussed how to train decision trees using the ID3 algorithm, which recursively splits the training instances into subsets that reduce our uncertainty about the value of the response variable. We used decision trees to predict whether or not an image on a web page is a banner advertisement. In the next chapter, we will introduce methods that model a relationship using collections of estimators.

9

From Decision Trees to Random Forests and Other Ensemble Methods

An **ensemble** is a combination of estimators that performs better than each of its components. In this chapter, we will introduce three methods of creating ensembles: **bagging**, **boosting**, and **stacking**. First, we will apply bagging to the decision trees introduced in the previous chapter to create a powerful ensemble called **random forest**. Then we will introduce boosting and the popular **AdaBoost** algorithm. Finally, we will use stacking to create ensembles from heterogeneous base estimators.

Bagging

Bootstrap aggregating, or bagging, is an ensemble meta-algorithm that can reduce the variance in an estimator. Bagging can be used in classification and regression tasks. When the component estimators are regressors, the ensemble averages their predictions. When the component estimators are classifiers, the ensemble returns the mode class.

Bagging independently fits multiple models on variants of the training data. The training data variants are created using a procedure called **bootstrap resampling**. Often it is necessary to estimate a parameter of an unknown probability distribution using only a sample of the distribution. We can use this sample to calculate a statistic, but we know that this statistic will vary according to the sample we happened to draw. Bootstrap resampling is a method of estimating the uncertainty in a statistic. It can only be used if the observations in the sample are drawn independently. Bootstrap resampling produces multiple variants of the sample by repeatedly resampling with replacement from the original sample. All of the variant samples will have the same number of observations as the original sample, and may include any observation zero or more times. We can compute our statistics for each of these variants, and use these statistics to estimate the uncertainty in our estimate by creating a confidence interval or calculating the standard error. Let's work through an example:

```python
# In[1]:
import numpy as np

# Sample 10 integers
sample = np.random.randint(low=1, high=100, size=10)
print('Original sample: %s' % sample)
print('Sample mean: %s' % sample.mean())

# Bootstrap re-sample 100 times by re-sampling with replacement
  from the original sample
resamples = [np.random.choice(sample, size=sample.shape) for i in
  range(100)]
print('Number of bootstrap re-samples: %s' % len(resamples))
print('Example re-sample: %s' % resamples[0])

resample_means = np.array([resample.mean() for resample in
  resamples])
print('Mean of re-samples\' means: %s' % resample_means.mean())

# Out[1]:
Original sample: [60 84 64 59 58 30  1 97 58 34]
Sample mean: 54.5
Number of bootstrap re-samples: 100
Example re-sample: [30 59 97 58 60 84 58 34 64 58]
Mean of re-samples' means: 54.183
```

Bagging is a useful meta-algorithm for estimators that have high variance and low bias, such as decision trees. In fact, bagged decision tree ensembles are used so often and successfully that the combination has its own name: the random forest. The number of trees in the forest is an important hyperparameter. Increasing the number of trees improves the model's performance at the cost of computational complexity. Regularization techniques, such as pruning or requiring a minimum number of training instances per leaf node, are less important when training trees for forests than they are for training a single estimator, as bagging provides regularization. In addition to bagging, learning algorithms for random forests often differ from their counterparts for trees in a second way. Recall from the previous chapter that decision tree learning algorithms such as ID3 construct trees by choosing the feature that produces the best split at each node, as measured by information gain or Gini impurity. For random forests, the algorithm selects the best from only a random sample of the features at each node. Let's train a random forest with scikit-learn:

```
# In[1]:
from sklearn.tree import DecisionTreeClassifier
from sklearn.ensemble import RandomForestClassifier
from sklearn.datasets import make_classification
from sklearn.model_selection import train_test_split
from sklearn.metrics import classification_report

X, y = make_classification(
  n_samples=1000, n_features=100, n_informative=20,
  n_clusters_per_class=2,
  random_state=11)
X_train, X_test, y_train, y_test = train_test_split(X, y,
  random_state=11)

clf = DecisionTreeClassifier(random_state=11)
clf.fit(X_train, y_train)
predictions = clf.predict(X_test)
print(classification_report(y_test, predictions))
```

```
# Out[1]:
             precision    recall  f1-score    support

          0       0.73      0.66      0.69        127
          1       0.68      0.75      0.71        123

avg / total       0.71      0.70      0.70        250
```

```
# In[2]:
clf = RandomForestClassifier(n_estimators=10, random_state=11)
clf.fit(X_train, y_train)
predictions = clf.predict(X_test)
print(classification_report(y_test, predictions))
```

```
# Out[2]:
            precision     recall   f1-score    support

        0       0.74       0.83       0.79        127
        1       0.80       0.70       0.75        123

avg / total     0.77       0.77       0.77        250
```

First, we use `make_classificaton` to create an artificial classification dataset. This convenience function allows fine-grained control over the characteristics of the dataset it produces. We create a dataset with *1,000* instances. Of the 100 features, 20 are informative; the remainder are redundant combinations of the information features, or noise. We then train and evaluate a single decision tree, followed by a random forest with 10 trees. The random forest's F1 precision, recall, and F1 scores are greater.

Boosting

Boosting is a family of ensemble methods that are primarily used to reduce the bias of an estimator. Boosting can be used in classification and regression tasks. Like bagging, boosting creates ensembles of homogeneous estimators. We will focus our discussion of boosting on one of the most popular boosting algorithms, AdaBoost.

AdaBoost is an iterative algorithm that was formulated by Yoav Freund and Robert Schapire in 1995. It's name is a portmanteau of **adaptive boosting**. On the first iteration, AdaBoost assigns equal weights to all of the training instances and then trains a weak learner. A **weak learner** (or weak classifier, weak predictor, and so on), is defined only as an estimator that performs slightly better than random chance, such as a decision tree with one or a small number of nodes. Weak learners are often, but not necessarily, simple models. A **strong learner**, in contrast, is defined as an estimator that is arbitrarily better than a weak learner. Most boosting algorithms, including AdaBoost, can use any base estimator as a weak learner. On subsequent iterations, AdaBoost increases the weights of training instances that the previous iteration's weak learner predicted incorrectly and decreases the weights of the instances that were predicted correctly. It then trains another weak learner on the re-weighted instances. Subsequent learners increasingly focus on instances that the ensemble predicts incorrectly. The algorithm terminates when it achieves perfect performance, or after a specified number of iterations. The ensemble predicts the weighted sum of the base estimators' predictions.

scikit-learn implements a variety of boosting meta-estimators for classification and regression tasks, including AdaBoostClassifier, AdaBoostRegressor, GradientBoostingClassifier, and GradientBoostingRegressor. In the following example, we train an AdaBoostClassifier for an artificial dataset created using the make_classification convenience function. We then plot the accuracy of the ensemble as the number of base estimators increases. We compare the ensemble's accuracy with the accuracy of a single decision tree:

```
# In[1]:
%matplotlib inline

# In[2]:
from sklearn.ensemble import AdaBoostClassifier
from sklearn.tree import DecisionTreeClassifier
from sklearn.datasets import make_classification
from sklearn.model_selection import train_test_split
import matplotlib.pyplot as plt

X, y = make_classification(
  n_samples=1000, n_features=50, n_informative=30,
  n_clusters_per_class=3,
  random_state=11)
X_train, X_test, y_train, y_test = train_test_split(X, y, random_state=11)

clf = DecisionTreeClassifier(random_state=11)
clf.fit(X_train, y_train)
print('Decision tree accuracy: %s' % clf.score(X_test, y_test))

# Out[2]:
Decision tree accuracy: 0.688

# In[3]:
# When an argument for the base_estimator parameter is not passed, the
default DecisionTreeClassifier is used
clf = AdaBoostClassifier(n_estimators=50, random_state=11)
clf.fit(X_train, y_train)
accuracies.append(clf.score(X_test, y_test))

plt.title('Ensemble Accuracy')
plt.ylabel('Accuracy')
plt.xlabel('Number of base estimators in ensemble')
plt.plot(range(1, 51), [accuracy for accuracy in clf.staged_score(X_test,
y_test)])
```

The code sample generates the following plot:

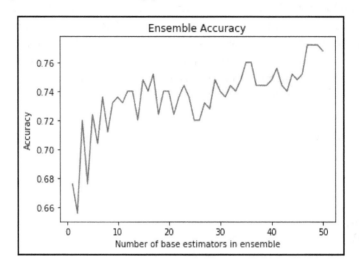

Stacking

Stacking is an approach to creating ensembles; it uses a meta-estimator to combine the predictions of base estimators. Sometimes called **blending**, stacking adds a second supervised learning problem: the meta-estimator must be trained to use the predictions of the base estimators to predict the value of the response variable. To train a stacked ensemble, first use the training set to train the base estimators. Unlike bagging and boosting, stacking can use different types of base estimators; a random forest could be combined with a logistic regression classifier, for example. The base estimators' predictions and the ground truth are then used as the training set for the meta-estimator. The meta-estimator can learn to combine the base estimators' predictions in more complex ways than voting or averaging. scikit-learn does not implement a stacking meta-estimator, but we can extend the `BaseEstimator` class to create our own. In this example, we use a single decision tree as the meta-estimator; the base estimators are a logistic regression classifier and a KNN classifier. Rather than using the predicted class labels as features, we use the predicted probabilities of the classes. Again, we create an artificial classification dataset using `make_classification`. We then train and evaluate the individual base estimators. Finally, we train and evaluate the ensemble, which has better accuracy:

```
# In[1]:
import numpy as np
from sklearn.model_selection import train_test_split
from sklearn.neighbors import KNeighborsClassifier
```

```
from sklearn.tree import DecisionTreeClassifier
from sklearn.linear_model import LogisticRegression
from sklearn.datasets import make_classification
from sklearn.base import clone, BaseEstimator, TransformerMixin,
  ClassifierMixin


class StackingClassifier(BaseEstimator, ClassifierMixin,
  TransformerMixin):

    def __init__(self, classifiers):
        self.classifiers = classifiers
        self.meta_classifier = DecisionTreeClassifier()

    def fit(self, X, y):
        for clf in self.classifiers:
            clf.fit(X, y)
        self.meta_classifier.fit(self._get_meta_features(X), y)
        return self

    def _get_meta_features(self, X):
        probas = np.asarray([clf.predict_proba(X) for clf in
          self.classifiers])
        return np.concatenate(probas, axis=1)

    def predict(self, X):
        return self.meta_classifier.predict(self._get_meta_features(X))

    def predict_proba(self, X):
        return
self.meta_classifier.predict_proba(self._get_meta_features(X))


X, y = make_classification(
    n_samples=1000, n_features=50, n_informative=30,
      n_clusters_per_class=3,
      random_state=11)
X_train, X_test, y_train, y_test = train_test_split(X, y,
    random_state=11)

lr = LogisticRegression()
lr.fit(X_train, y_train)
print('Logistic regression accuracy: %s' % lr.score(X_test,
    y_test))

knn_clf = KNeighborsClassifier()
knn_clf.fit(X_train, y_train)
print('KNN accuracy: %s' % knn_clf.score(X_test, y_test))
```

```
# Out[1]:
Logistic regression accuracy: 0.816
KNN accuracy: 0.836

# In[2]:
base_classifiers = [lr, knn_clf]
stacking_clf = StackingClassifier(base_classifiers)
stacking_clf.fit(X_train, y_train)
print('Stacking classifier accuracy: %s' % stacking_clf.score(X_test,
y_test))

# Out[2]:
Stacking classifier accuracy: 0.852
```

Summary

In this chapter, we introduced ensembles. An ensemble is a combination of models that performs better than each of its components. We discussed three methods of training ensembles. Bootstrap aggregating, or bagging, can reduce the variance of an estimator; bagging uses bootstrap resampling to create multiple variants of the training set. The predictions of models trained on these variants are then averaged. Bagged decision trees are called random forests. Boosting is an ensemble meta-estimator that reduces the bias of its base estimators. AdaBoost is a popular boosting algorithm that iteratively trains estimators on training data that is weighted according to the previous estimators' errors. Finally, in stacking a meta-estimator learns to combine the predictions of heterogeneous base estimators.

10
The Perceptron

In previous chapters, we discussed linear models such as multiple linear regression and logistic regression. In this chapter, we will introduce another linear model for binary classification tasks called the **perceptron**. While the perceptron is seldom used today, understanding it and its limitations is important in order to understand the models that we will discuss in the following chapters.

The perceptron

Invented by Frank Rosenblatt at the Cornell Aeronautical Laboratory in the late 1950s, the development of the perceptron was originally motivated by efforts to simulate the human brain. A brain is composed of cells called **neurons** that process information, and connections between neurons are called **synapses**, through which information is transmitted. The human brain has been estimated to be composed of as many as *100* billion neurons and *100* trillion synapses. Illustrated in the following image, the main components of a neuron are dendrites, a body, and an axon. The dendrites receive electrical signals from other neurons. The signals are processed in the neuron's body, which then sends a signal through the axon to another neuron.

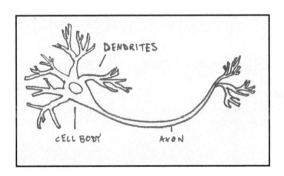

An individual neuron can be thought of as a computational unit that processes one or more inputs to produce an output. A perceptron functions analogously to a neuron; it accepts one or more inputs, processes them, and returns an output. It may seem that a model of just one of the hundreds of billions of neurons in the human brain will be of limited use. To some extent, that is true; a single perceptron is incapable of approximating many functions. However, we will still discuss perceptrons for two reasons. First, perceptrons are capable of online learning; the learning algorithm can update the model's parameters using a single training instance rather than the entire batch of training instances. Online learning is useful for learning from training sets that are too large to be represented in memory. Second, understanding the perceptron and its limitations is necessary for understanding some of the more powerful models that we will discuss in subsequent chapters, including support vector machines and artificial neural networks. Perceptrons are commonly visualized using a diagram like the following:

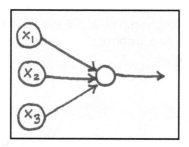

The circles labeled x_1, x_2, and x_3 are input units. Each input unit represents one feature. Perceptrons frequently use an additional input unit that represents a constant bias term, but this input unit is usually omitted from diagrams. The circle in the center is a computational unit, or the neuron's body. The edges connecting the input units to the computational unit are analogous to dendrites. Each edge is associated with a parameter, or weight. The parameters can be interpreted easily; a feature that is correlated with the positive class will have a positive weight, and a feature that is correlated with the negative class will have a negative weight. The edge directed away from the computational unit returns the output, and can be thought of as the axon.

Activation functions

The perceptron classifies instances by processing a linear combination of the features and the model parameters using an activation function, as shown in the following equation:

$$y = \phi \left(\sum_{i=1}^{n} w_i x_i + b \right)$$

Here, w_i are the model's parameters, b is a constant bias term, and ϕ is the activation function. The linear combination of the parameters and inputs is sometimes called **preactivation**. Several different activation functions are commonly used. Rosenblatt's original perceptron used the **Heaviside step function**. Also called the **unit step function**, the Heaviside step function is shown in the following equation, where x is the weighted combination of the features:

$$g(x) = \begin{cases} 1, & \text{if } x > 0 \\ 0, & \text{elsewhere} \end{cases}$$

If the weighted sum of the features and the bias term is greater than 0, the activation function returns 1 and the perceptron predicts that the instance is the positive class. Otherwise, the function returns 0 and the perceptron predicts that the instance is the negative class. The Heaviside step activation function is plotted in the following figure:

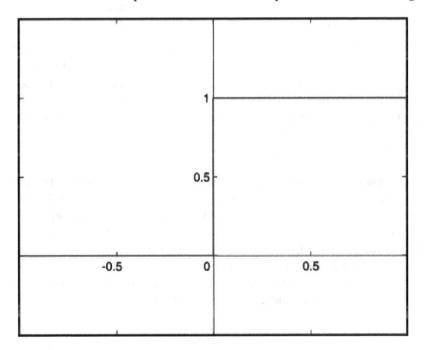

Another common activation function is the logistic sigmoid:

$$g(x) = \frac{1}{1 + e^{-x}}$$

x is the weighted sum of the inputs. Unlike the unit step function, the logistic sigmoid is differentiable; this difference will become important when we discuss artificial neural networks.

The perceptron learning algorithm

The perceptron learning algorithm begins by setting the weights to zero, or to small random values. It then predicts the class for a training instance. The perceptron is an error-driven learning algorithm; if the prediction is correct, the algorithm continues to the next instance. If the prediction is incorrect, the algorithm updates the weights. More formally, the update rule is given by the following:

$$w_i(t + 1) = w_i(t) + a(d_j - y_j(t))x_{j,i}, \text{ for all feature } 0 \leq i \leq n.$$

For each training instance, the value of the parameter for each feature is incremented by $a(d_j - y_j(t))x_{j,i}$, where d_j is the true class for instance j, $y_j(t)$ is the predicted class for instance j, $x_{j,i}$ is the value of the ith feature for instance j, and a is a hyperparameter that controls the learning rate. If the prediction is correct, $d_j - y_j(t)$ equals zero, and the term $a(d_j - y_j(t))x_{j,i}$ equals zero. That is, if the prediction is correct, the weight is not updated. If the prediction is incorrect, we compute the product of $d_j - y_j(t)$, the value of the feature, and the learning rate. We then add the product (which may be negative) to the weight.

This update rule is similar to the update rule for gradient descent in that the weights are adjusted towards classifying the instance correctly and the size of the update is controlled by a learning rate. Each pass through the training instances is called an **epoch**. The learning algorithm has converged when it completes an epoch without misclassifying any of the instances. The learning algorithm is not guaranteed to converge; later in the chapter, we will discuss linearly inseparable datasets for which convergence is impossible. For this reason, the learning algorithm also requires a hyperparameter that specifies the maximum number of epochs that can be completed before the algorithm terminates.

Binary classification with the perceptron

Let's work through a toy classification problem. Suppose that you wish to separate adult cats from kittens. Only two explanatory variables are available in your dataset: the proportion of the day when the animal was asleep and the proportion of the day when the animal was grumpy. Our training data consists of the following four instances:

Instance	Proportion of the day spent sleeping	Proportion of the day spent being grumpy	Kitten or adult?
1	0.2	0.1	Kitten
2	0.4	0.6	Kitten
3	0.5	0.2	Kitten
4	0.7	0.9	Adult

The following scatter plot of the instances confirms that they are linearly separable:

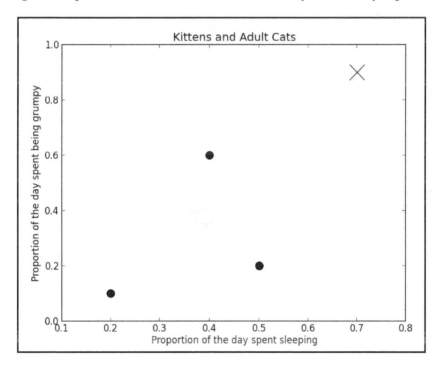

Our goal is to train a perceptron that can classify animals using the two real-valued features. We will represent kittens with the positive class and adult cats with the negative class. Our perceptron has three input units. x_1 is the input unit for the bias term. x_2 and x_3 are input units for the two features. Our perceptron's computational unit uses the unit step activation function. In this example, we will set the maximum number of training epochs to ten; if the algorithm does not converge within ten epochs, it will stop and return the current values of the weights. For simplicity, we will set the learning rate to 1. Initially, we will set all of the weights to 0. Let's examine the first training epoch, which is shown in the following table:

Instance	Initial weights; x; Activation	Prediction, Target	Is correct?	Updated weights
0	0, 0, 0; 1.0, 0.2, 0.1; 1.0*0 + 0.2*0 + 0.1*0 = 0.0;	0, 1	False	1.0, 0.2, 0.1
1	1.0, 0.2, 0.1; 1.0, 0.4, 0.6; 1.0*1.0 + 0.4*0.2 + 0.6*0.1 = 1.14;	1, 1	True	No update
2	1.0, 0.2, 0.1; 1.0, 0.5, 0.2; 1.0*1.0 + 0.5*0.2 + 0.2*0.1 = 1.12;	1, 1	True	No update
3	1.0, 0.2, 0.1; 1.0, 0.7, 0.9; 1.0*1.0 + 0.7*0.2 + 0.9*0.1 = 1.23;	1, 0	False	0, -0.5, -0.8

Initially, all of the weights are equal to zero. The weighted sum of the features for the first instance is zero, the activation function outputs zero, and the perceptron incorrectly predicts that the kitten is an adult cat. Because the prediction is incorrect, we update the weights according to the update rule. We increment each of the weights by the product of the learning rate (*1*), the difference between the true and predicted labels (*1*), and the value of the corresponding feature.

We then continue to the second training instance and calculate the weighted sum of its features using the updated weights. This sum equals *1.14*, so the activation function outputs *1*. This prediction is correct, so we continue to the third training instance without updating the weights. The prediction for the third instance is also correct, so we continue to the fourth training instance. The weighted sum of the features for the fourth instance is *1.23*. The activation function outputs *1*, incorrectly predicting that this adult cat is a kitten. Since this prediction is incorrect, we increment each weight by the product of the learning rate, the difference between the true and predicted labels, and its corresponding feature. We have completed the first epoch by classifying all of the instances in the training set. The perceptron did not converge; it classified half of the training instances incorrectly. The following figure depicts the decision boundary after the first epoch:

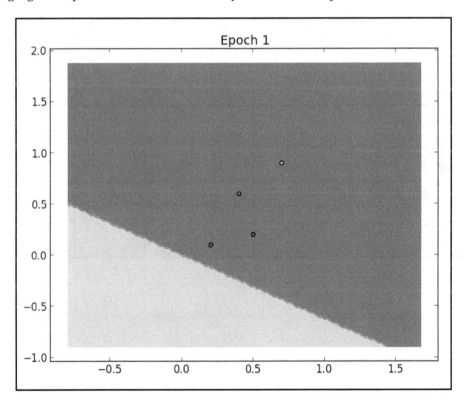

Note that the decision boundary moved throughout the epoch; the decision boundary formed by the weights at the end of the epoch would not necessarily have produced the same predictions seen earlier in the epoch. Since we have not exceeded the maximum number of training epochs, we will iterate through the instances again. The second training epoch is shown in the following table:

Instance	Initial weights; x; Activation	Prediction, target	Is correct?	Updated weights
0	0, -0.5, -0.8 1.0, 0.2, 0.1 1.0*0 + 0.2*-0.5 + 0.1*-0.8 = -0.18	0, 1	False	1, -0.3, -0.7
1	1, -0.3, -0.7 1.0, 0.4, 0.6 1.0*1.0 + 0.4*-0.3 + 0.6*-0.7 = 0.46	1, 1	True	1, -0.3, -0.7
2	1, -0.3, -0.7 1.0, 0.5, 0.2 1.0*1.0 + 0.5*-0.3 + 0.2*-0.7 = 0.71	1, 1	True	1, -0.3, -0.7
3	1, -0.3, -0.7 1.0, 0.7, 0.9 1.0*1.0 + 0.7*-0.3 + 0.9*-0.7 = 0.16	1, 0	False	0, -1, -1.6

The second epoch begins using the values of the weights from the first epoch. Two training instances are classified incorrectly during this epoch. The weights are updated twice, but the decision boundary at the end of the second epoch is similar the decision boundary at the end of the first epoch:

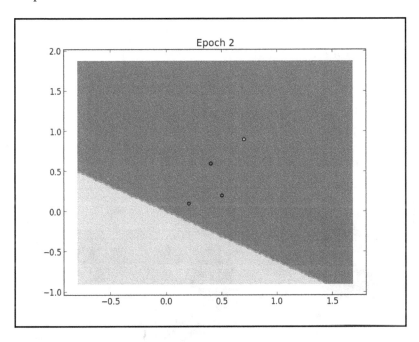

The algorithm failed to converge during this epoch, so we will continue training. The following table describes the third training epoch.

Instance	Initial weights; x; activation	Prediction, target	Is correct?	Updated weights
0	0, -1, -1.6 1.0, 0.2, 0.1 1.0*0 + 0.2*-1.0 + 0.1*-1.6 = -0.36	0, 1	False	1,-0.8, -1.5
1	1,-0.8, -1.5 1.0, 0.4, 0.6 1.0*1.0 + 0.4*-0.8 + 0.6*-1.5 = -0.22	0, 1	False	2, -0.4, -0.9

| 2 | 2, -0.4, -0.9
1.0, 0.5, 0.2
1.0*2.0 + 0.5*-0.4 + 0.2*-0.9 =
1.62 | 1, 1 | *True* | 2, -0.4, -0.9 |
| 3 | 2, -0.4, -0.9
1.0, 0.7, 0.9
1.0*2.0 + 0.7*-0.4 + 0.9*-0.9 =
0.91 | 1, 0 | *False* | 1, -1.1, -1.8 |

The perceptron classifies more instances incorrectly during this epoch than during previous epochs. The following figure depicts the decision boundary at the end of the third epoch. Again, note that the because the weights are updated after each training instance is classified, the decision boundary is different throughout the epoch:

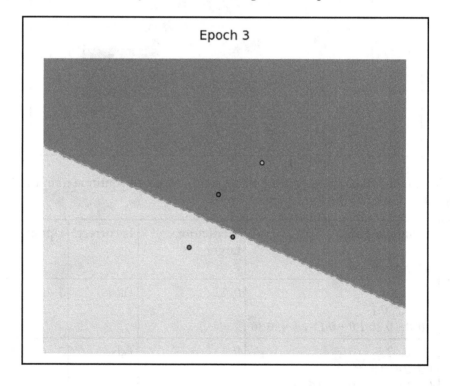

The perceptron continues to update its weights throughout the fourth and fifth training epochs, and continues to classify training instances incorrectly. During the sixth epoch, the perceptron classified all of the instances correctly; it converged on a set of weights that separates the two classes. The following table describes the sixth training epoch:

Instance	Initial Weights; x; Activation	Prediction, target	Is correct?	Updated weights
0	2, -1, -1.5 1.0, 0.2, 0.1 1.0*2 + 0.2*-1 + 0.1*-1.5 = 1.65	1, 1	True	2, -1, -1.5
1	2, -1, -1.5 1.0, 0.4, 0.6 1.0*2 + 0.4*-1 + 0.6*-1.5 = 0.70	1, 1	True	2, -1, -1.5
2	2, -1, -1.5 1.0, 0.5, 0.2 1.0*2 + 0.5*-1 + 0.2*-1.5 = 1.2	1, 1	True	2, -1, -1.5
3	2, -1, -1.5 1.0, 0.7, 0.9 1.0*2 + 0.7*-1 + 0.9*-1.5 = -0.05	0, 0	True	2, -1, -1.5

The decision boundary at the end of the sixth training epoch is visualized in the following figure:

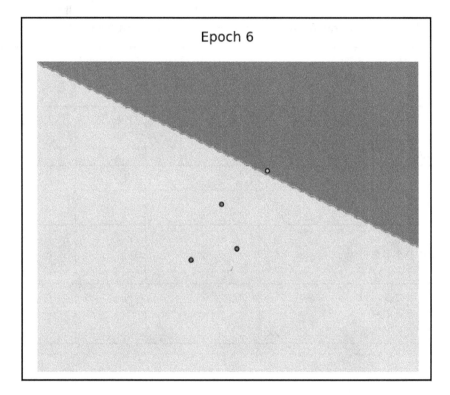

The following figure visualizes the decision boundary throughout the previous training epochs:

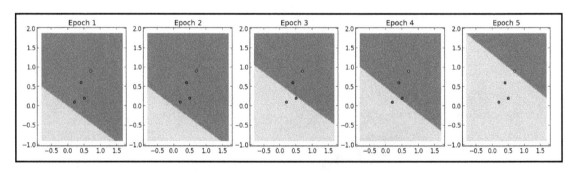

Document classification with the perceptron

Like other estimators, the `Perceptron` class implements `fit` and `predict` methods and hyperparameters are specified through its constructor. `Perceptron` also implements a `partial_fit` method, which allows the classifier to be trained incrementally.

In this example, we train a perceptron to classify documents from the 20 Newsgroups dataset. The dataset consists of approximately *20,000* documents sampled from 20 Usenet newsgroups. The dataset is commonly used in document classification and clustering experiments; scikit-learn even provides a convenience function for downloading and reading the dataset. We will train a perceptron to classify documents from three newsgroups: `rec.sports.hockey`, `rec.sports.baseball`, and `rec.auto`. Perceptron is capable of multiclass classification; it will use the one-versus-all strategy to train a classifier for each of the classes in the training data. We will represent the documents as tf-idf-weighted bags-of-words. The `partial_fit` method can be used in conjunction with `HashingVectorizer` to train from large or streaming data in a memory-constrained setting:

```
# In[1]:
from sklearn.datasets import fetch_20newsgroups
from sklearn.feature_extraction.text import TfidfVectorizer
from sklearn.linear_model import Perceptron
from sklearn.metrics import f1_score, classification_report

categories = ['rec.sport.hockey', 'rec.sport.baseball',
    'rec.autos']
newsgroups_train = fetch_20newsgroups(subset='train',
    categories=categories, remove=('headers', 'footers', 'quotes'))
newsgroups_test = fetch_20newsgroups(subset='test',
    categories=categories, remove=('headers', 'footers', 'quotes'))

vectorizer = TfidfVectorizer()
X_train = vectorizer.fit_transform(newsgroups_train.data)
X_test = vectorizer.transform(newsgroups_test.data)
clf = Perceptron(random_state=11)
clf.fit(X_train, newsgroups_train.target )
predictions = clf.predict(X_test)
print(classification_report(newsgroups_test.target, predictions))

# Out[1]:
           precision    recall  f1-score   support

        0       0.81      0.92      0.86       396
        1       0.87      0.76      0.81       397
        2       0.86      0.85      0.86       399
```

```
avg / total        0.85       0.84      0.84       1192
```

First we download and read the dataset using the `fetch_20newsgroups` function. Consistent with other built-in datasets, the function returns an object with `data`, `target`, and `target_names` attributes. We also specify that the documents' headers, footers, and quotes should be removed. Each of the newsgroups used different formatting conventions in the headers and footers; retaining them makes classifying the documents artificially easy. We produce tf-idf vectors using the `TfifdVectorizer`, train the perceptron, and evaluate it on the test set. Without hyperparameter optimization, the perceptron's average precision, recall, and F1 score are `0.84`.

Limitations of the perceptron

The perceptron uses a hyperplane to separate the positive and negative classes. A simple example of a classification problem that is linearly inseparable is the logical exclusive disjunction, or XOR. The output of XOR is *1* when one of its inputs is equal to *1* and the other is equal to *0*. Otherwise, the output is *0*. The inputs and outputs of XOR are plotted in two dimensions in the following graph. When XOR outputs **1**, the instance is marked with a circle; when XOR outputs **0**, the instance is marked with a diamond:

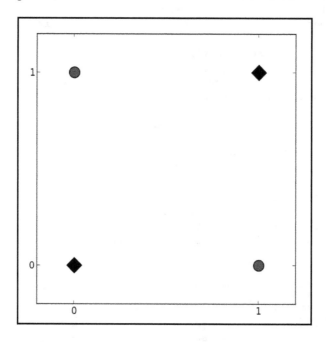

It is impossible to separate the circles from the diamonds using a single straight line.

Suppose that the instances are pegs on a board. If you were to stretch a rubber band around both of the positive instances, and stretch a second rubber band around both of the negative instances, the bands would intersect in the middle of the board. The rubber bands represent **convex hulls**, or the envelope that contains all the points within the set and all the points along any line connecting a pair points within the set. Feature representations are more likely to be linearly separable in higher dimensional spaces than lower dimensional spaces. For instance, text classification problems tend to be linearly separable when high-dimensional representations such as the bag-of-words are used.

In the next two chapters, we will discuss techniques that can be used to model linearly inseparable data. The first technique, called **kernelization**, projects linearly inseparable data to a higher dimensional space in which it is linearly separable. Kernelization can be used in many models, including perceptrons, but it is particularly associated with support vector machines, which we will discuss in the next chapter. The second technique creates a directed graph of perceptrons. The resulting model, called an **Artificial Neural Network (ANN)**, is a universal function approximator; we will discuss artificial neural networks in Chapter 12, *From the Perceptron to Artificial Neural Networks*.

Summary

In this chapter, we discussed the perceptron. Inspired by neurons, the perceptron is linear model for binary classification. The perceptron classifies instances by processing a linear combination of features and weights with an activation function. While a perceptron with a logistic sigmoid activation function is the same model as logistic regression, the perceptron learns its weights using an online, error-driven algorithm. The perceptron can be used effectively in some problems. Like the other linear classifiers that we have discussed, the perceptron separates the instances of positive and negative classes using a hyperplane. Some datasets are not linearly separable; that is, no possible hyperplane can classify all the instances correctly.

In the following chapters, we will discuss two models that can be used with linearly inseparable data: ANN, which creates a universal function approximator from a graph of perceptrons, and the support vector machine, which projects the data onto a higher dimensional space in which it is linearly separable.

11
From the Perceptron to Support Vector Machines

In the previous chapter, we introduced the perceptron and described why it cannot effectively classify linearly inseparable data. Recall that we encountered a similar problem in our discussion on multiple linear regression; we examined a dataset in which the response variable was not linearly related to the explanatory variables. To improve the accuracy of the model, we introduced a special case of multiple linear regression called **polynomial regression**. We created synthetic combinations of features, and we were able to model a linear relationship between the response variable and the features in the higher dimensional feature space.

While this method of increasing the dimensions of the feature space may seem like a promising technique to use when approximating nonlinear functions with linear models, it suffers from two related problems. The first is a computational problem; computing the mapped features and working with larger vectors requires more computing power. The second problem pertains to generalization; increasing the dimensions of the feature representation exacerbates the curse of dimensionality. Learning from high-dimensional feature representations requires exponentially more training data to avoid overfitting.

In this chapter, we will discuss a powerful discriminative model for classification and regression, called the **support vector machine (SVM)**. First we will revisit mapping features to higher dimensional spaces. Then we will discuss how SVMs mitigate the computation and generalization problems encountered when learning from data mapped to high-dimensional spaces. Entire books are devoted to describing SVMs, and describing the optimization algorithms used to train SVMs requires more advanced math than we have used in previous chapters. Instead of working through simple examples in detail as we did in previous chapters, we will try to develop an intuition of how SVMs work in order to apply them effectively with scikit-learn.

Kernels and the kernel trick

Recall that the perceptron separates instances of the positive class from instances of the negative class using a hyperplane as a decision boundary. The decision boundary is given by the following formula:

$$f(x) = \langle w, x \rangle + b$$

Predictions are made using the following function:

$$h(x) = \text{sign}(f(x))$$

 Note that we previously indicated the inner product $\langle w, x \rangle$ with wTx. To be consistent with the notational conventions used for SVM, we will adopt the former in this chapter.

While the proof is beyond the scope of this chapter, we can write the model differently. The following expression of the model is called the **dual** form. The expression we used previously is the **primal** form.

$$f(x) = \langle w, x \rangle + b = \sum \alpha_i y_i \langle x_i, x \rangle + b$$

The most important difference between the primal and dual forms is that the primal form computes the inner product of the model parameters and the test instance's feature vector, while the dual form computes the inner product of the training instance's and the test instance's feature vector. Shortly we will exploit this property of the dual form to work with linearly inseparable classes. First, we must formalize our definition of mapping features to higher dimensional spaces.

In the section on *Polynomial regression* from Chapter 5, *Simple Linear Regression to Multiple Linear Regression*, we mapped features to a higher dimensional space in which they were linearly related to the response variable. The mapping increased the number of features by creating quadratic terms from combinations of the original features. These synthetic features allowed us to express a nonlinear function with a linear model. In general, a mapping is given by the following:

$$x \to \phi(x)$$
$$\phi : R^d \to R^D$$

The plot on the left in the following figure shows the original feature space of a linearly inseparable dataset. The plot on the right shows that the data is linearly separable after mapping to a higher dimensional space:

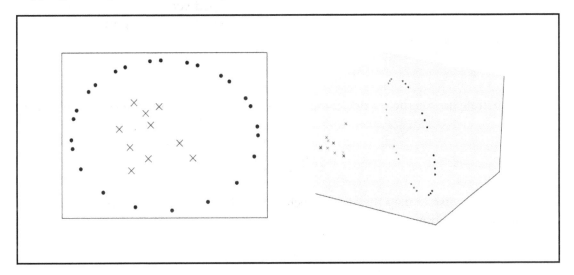

Let's return to the dual form of our decision boundary and the observation that the feature vectors appear only inside of a dot product. We can map the data to a higher dimensional space by applying the mapping to the feature vectors, as follows:

$$f(x) = \sum \alpha_i y_i \langle x_i, x \rangle + b$$

$$f(x) = \sum \alpha_i y_i \langle \phi(x_i), \phi(x) \rangle + b$$

As noted, this mapping allows us to express more complex models, but it introduces computation and generalization problems. Mapping the feature vectors and computing their dot products can require a prohibitively large amount of processing power.

Observe in the second equation that while we have mapped the feature vectors to a higher dimensional space, the feature vectors still only appear as a dot product. The dot product is a scalar; we do not require the mapped feature vectors once this scalar has been computed. If we can use a different method to produce the same scalar as the dot product of the mapped vectors, we can avoid the costly work of explicitly computing the dot product and mapping the feature vectors.

Fortunately, there is a method called **kernel trick**. A **kernel** is a function that, given the original feature vectors, returns the same value as the dot product of its corresponding mapped feature vectors. Kernels do not explicitly map the feature vectors to a higher dimensional space or calculate the dot product of the mapped vectors. Kernels produce the same value through a different series of operations that can often be computed more efficiently. Kernels are defined more formally in the following equation:

$$K(x, z) = \langle \phi(x), \phi(z) \rangle$$

Let's demonstrate how kernels work. Suppose that we have two feature vectors, x and z:

$$x = (x_1, x_2)$$

$$z = (z_1, z_2)$$

In our model, we wish to map the feature vectors to a higher dimensional space using the following transformation:

$$\phi(x) = x^2$$

The dot product of the mapped, normalized feature vectors is equivalent to:

$$\langle \phi(x), \phi(z) \rangle = \langle (x_1^2, x_2^2, \sqrt{2}x_1x_2), (z_1^2, z_2^2, \sqrt{2}z_1z_2) \rangle$$

The kernel given by the following formula produces the same value as the dot product of the mapped feature vectors:

$$K(x, z) = \langle x, z \rangle^2 = (x_1z_1 + x_2z_2)^2 = x_1^2z_1^2 + 2x_1z_1x_2z_2 + x_2^2z_2^2$$

$$K(x, z) = \langle \phi(x), \phi(z) \rangle$$

Let's plug in values for the feature vectors to make this example more concrete:

$$x = (4, 9)$$
$$z = (3, 3)$$
$$K(x, z) = 4^2 \times 3^2 + 2 \times 4 \times 3 \times 9 \times 3 + 9^2 \times 3^2 = 1521$$
$$\langle \emptyset(x), \emptyset(z) \rangle = \left\langle \left(4^2, 9^2, \sqrt{2} \times 4 \times 9 \right), \left(3^2, 3^2, \sqrt{2}, \times 3 \times 3 \right) \right\rangle = 1521$$

The kernel $K(x, z)$ produced the same value as the dot product $\langle \phi(x), \phi(z) \rangle$ of the mapped feature vectors, but it never explicitly mapped the feature vectors to the higher dimensional space and required fewer arithmetic operations. This example used only two-dimensional feature vectors. Datasets with even a modest number of features can result in mapped feature spaces with massive dimensions. scikit-learn provides several commonly used kernels, including the polynomial, sigmoid, Gaussian, and linear kernels. Polynomial kernels are given by the following equation:

$$K\left(x, x'\right) = \left(\gamma \left\langle x - x' \right\rangle + r\right)^{k}$$

Quadratic kernels, or polynomial kernels where k is equal to 2, are commonly used in natural language processing. The sigmoid kernel is given by the following equation. γ and r are hyperparameters that can be tuned through cross-validation.

$$K\left(x, x'\right) = \tanh\left(\gamma \left\langle x - x' \right\rangle + r\right)$$

The Gaussian kernel is a good first choice for problems requiring nonlinear models. The Gaussian kernel is a **radial basis function**. A decision boundary that is a hyperplane in the mapped feature space is similar to a decision boundary that is a hypersphere in the original space. The feature space produced by the Gaussian kernel can have an infinite number of dimensions, a feat that would be impossible otherwise. The Gaussian kernel is given by the following equation:

$$K\left(x, x'\right) = \exp\left(-\gamma \left| x - x' \right|^{2}\right)$$

It is always important to scale the features when using SVMs, but feature scaling is especially important when using the Gaussian kernel. Choosing a kernel can be challenging. Ideally, a kernel will measure similarity between instances in a way that is useful to the task. While kernels are commonly used with SVMs, they can also be used with any model that can be expressed in terms of the dot product of two feature vectors, including logistic regression, perceptrons, and **principal component analysis** (**PCA**). In the next section, we will address the second problem caused by mapping to high-dimensional feature spaces: generalization.

Maximum margin classification and support vectors

The following figure depicts instances from two linearly separable classes and three possible decision boundaries. All of the decision boundaries separate the training instances of the positive class from the training instances of the negative class, and a perceptron can learn any of them. Which of these decision boundaries is most likely to perform best on test data?

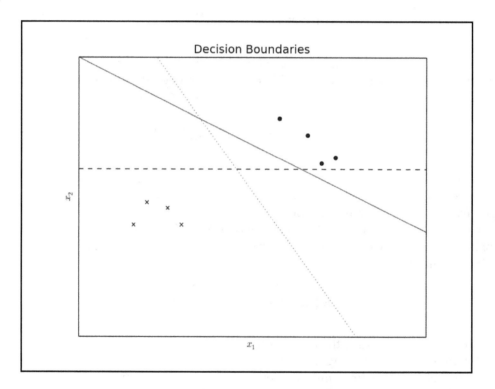

From this visualization, it is intuitive that the dotted decision boundary is the best. The solid decision boundary is near many of the positive instances. The test set could contain a positive instance that has a slightly smaller value for the first explanatory variable, x_1; this instance would be classified incorrectly. The dashed decision boundary is farther away from most of the training instances; however, it is near one of the positive instances and one of the negative instances.

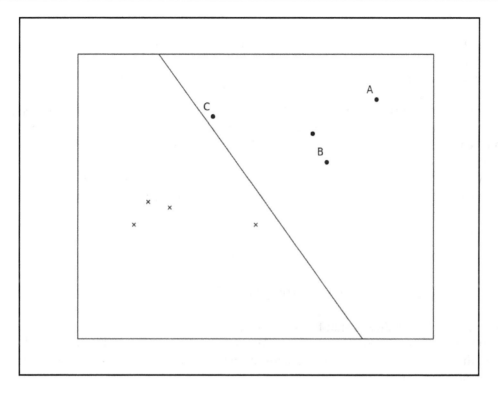

The previous figure provides a different perspective on evaluating decision boundaries. Assume that the line plotted is the decision boundary for a logistic regression classifier. The instance labeled **A** is far from the decision boundary; it would be predicted to belong to the positive class with a high probability. The instance labeled **B** would still be predicted to belong to the positive class, but the probability would be lower as the instance is closer to the decision boundary. Finally, the instance labeled **C** would be predicted to belong to the positive class with a low probability; even a small change to the training data could change the class that is predicted. The most confident predictions are for instances that are farthest from the decision boundary. We can estimate the confidence of the prediction using its functional margin. The functional margin of the training set is given by the following:

$$funct = \min \; y_i f(x_i)$$

$$f(x) = \langle w, x \rangle + b$$

Here, y_i is the true class of the instance. The functional margin is large for instance A and small for instance C. If C were misclassified, the functional margin would be negative. The instances for which the functional margin is equal to *1* are called support vectors. These instances alone are sufficient for defining the decision boundary; the other instances are not required to predict the class of a test instance. Related to the functional margin is the geometric margin, or the maximum width of the band that separates the support vectors. The geometric margin is equal to the normalized functional margin. It is necessary to normalize the functional margins as they can be scaled by w, which is problematic for training. When w is a unit vector, the geometric margin is equal to the functional vector. We can now formalize our definition of the best decision boundary as having the greatest geometric margin. The model parameters that maximize the geometric margin can be solved through the following constrained optimization problem:

$$min \frac{1}{2} \langle w, w \rangle$$

$$\text{subject to: } y_i(\langle w, x_i \rangle + b) \geq 1$$

A useful property of SVMs is that this optimization problem is convex; it has a single local minimum that is also the global minimum. While the proof is beyond the scope of this chapter, the previous optimization problem can be written using the dual form of the model to accommodate kernels, as follows:

$$W(\alpha) = \sum_i \alpha_i - \frac{1}{2} \sum_{i,j} \alpha_i \alpha_j y_i y_j K(x_i, x_j)$$

$$\text{subject to: } \sum_{i=1}^{n} y_i \alpha_i = 0$$

$$\text{subject to: } \alpha_i \geq 0$$

Finding the parameters that maximize the geometric margin is a quadratic programming problem. This problem is commonly solved using an algorithm called **Sequential Minimal Optimization (SMO)**. The SMO algorithm breaks the optimization problem down into a series of the smallest possible sub-problems, which are then solved analytically.

Classifying characters in scikit-learn

Let's apply SVMs to a classification problem. In recent years, SVMs have been used successfully in the task of character recognition. Given an image, the classifier must predict the character that is depicted. Character recognition is a component of many optical character recognition systems. Even small images require high-dimensional representations when raw pixel intensities are used as features. If the classes are linearly inseparable and must be mapped to a higher dimensional feature space, the dimensions of the feature space can become even larger. Fortunately, SVMs are suited to working with such data efficiently. First we will use scikit-learn to train a SVM to recognize handwritten digits. Then we will work on a more challenging problem: recognizing alphanumeric characters in photographs.

Classifying handwritten digits

The **Mixed National Institute of Standards and Technology** (**MNIST**) database is a collection of *70,000* images of handwritten digits. The digits were sampled from documents written by employees of the US Census Bureau and from American high school students. The images are grayscale and *28 x 28* pixels in dimension. Let's inspect some of the images using the following script:

```
# In[1]:
import matplotlib.pyplot as plt
from sklearn.datasets import fetch_mldata
import matplotlib.cm as cm

mnist = fetch_mldata('MNIST original', data_home='data/mnist')

counter = 1
for i in range(1, 4):
    for j in range(1, 6):
        plt.subplot(3, 5, counter)
        plt.imshow(mnist.data[(i - 1) * 8000 + j].reshape((28,
            28)), cmap=cm.Greys_r)
        plt.axis('off')
        counter += 1
plt.show()
```

First we load the data. scikit-learn provides the `fetch_mldata` convenience function for downloading the dataset if it is not found on disk and reading it into an object. Then we create a subplot for five instances for the digits 0, 1, and 2. The script produces the following image:

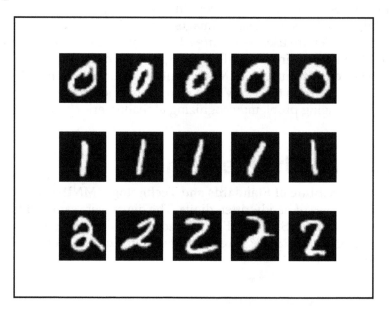

The MNIST dataset is partitioned into a training set of *60,000* images and a test set of *10,000* images. The dataset is commonly used to evaluate a variety of machine learning models; it is popular because little preprocessing is required. Let's use scikit-learn to build a classifier that can predict the digit that is depicted in an image:

```
# In[2]:
from sklearn.pipeline import Pipeline
from sklearn.preprocessing import scale
from sklearn.model_selection import train_test_split
from sklearn.svm import SVC
from sklearn.grid_search import GridSearchCV
from sklearn.metrics import classification_report

if __name__ == '__main__':
    X, y = mnist.data, mnist.target
    X = X/255.0*2 - 1
    X_train, X_test, y_train, y_test = train_test_split(X, y,
        random_state=11)

    pipeline = Pipeline([
        ('clf', SVC(kernel='rbf', gamma=0.01, C=100))
```

```
    ])

    parameters = {
        'clf__gamma': (0.01, 0.03, 0.1, 0.3, 1),
        'clf__C': (0.1, 0.3, 1, 3, 10, 30),
    }

    grid_search = GridSearchCV(pipeline, parameters, n_jobs=2,
        verbose=1, scoring='accuracy')
    grid_search.fit(X_train[:10000], y_train[:10000])
    print('Best score: %0.3f' % grid_search.best_score_)
    print('Best parameters set:')
    best_parameters = grid_search.best_estimator_.get_params()
    for param_name in sorted(parameters.keys()):
        print('\t%s: %r' % (param_name,
            best_parameters[param_name]))

    predictions = grid_search.predict(X_test)
    print(classification_report(y_test, predictions))

# Out[2]:
Fitting 3 folds for each of 30 candidates, totalling 90 fits
[Parallel(n_jobs=2)]: Done  46 tasks      | elapsed: 54.0min
[Parallel(n_jobs=2)]: Done  90 out of  90 | elapsed: 101.9min finished
Best score: 0.965
Best parameters set:
  clf__C: 3
 clf__gamma: 0.01
```

	precision	recall	f1-score	support
0.0	0.98	0.98	0.98	1770
1.0	0.99	0.98	0.98	1987
2.0	0.95	0.97	0.96	1738
3.0	0.96	0.96	0.96	1808
4.0	0.97	0.98	0.97	1703
5.0	0.96	0.96	0.96	1549
6.0	0.98	0.98	0.98	1677
7.0	0.98	0.96	0.97	1827
8.0	0.96	0.95	0.96	1701
9.0	0.96	0.96	0.96	1740
avg / total	0.97	0.97	0.97	17500

The script will fork additional processes during grid search, which requires execution from a __main__ block. First, we scale the features and center each feature around the origin. We then split the preprocessed data into training and test sets. Next we instantiate `SVC`, or support vector classifier, object. The `SVC` constructor has `kernel`, `gamma`, and `C` keyword arguments. The `kernel` keyword argument specifies the kernel to use. scikit-learn provides implementations of the linear, polynomial, sigmoid, and radial basis function kernels. The keyword argument `degree` should also be set when the polynomial kernel is used. `C` controls regularization; it is similar to the lambda hyperparameter we used for logistic regression. The keyword argument `gamma` is the kernel coefficient for the sigmoid, polynomial, and RBF kernels. Setting these hyperparameters can be challenging, so we tune them by grid searching. The best model has an average F1 Score of `0.97`; this score can be increased further by training on more than the first *10,000* instances.

Classifying characters in natural images

Now let's try a more challenging problem. We will classify alphanumeric characters in natural images. The Chars74K dataset contains more than *74,000* images of the digits 0 through 9 and the characters for both cases of the English alphabet. The following are three examples of images of the lowercase letter z.. Chars74K can be downloaded from `http://www.ee.surrey.ac.uk/CVSSP/demos/chars74k/`.

Several types of images comprise the collection. We will use *7,705* images of characters that were extracted from photographs of street scenes taken in Bangalore, India. In contrast to MNIST, the images in this portion of Chars74K depict the characters in a variety of fonts, colors, and perturbations. After expanding the archive, we will use the files in the directory called `English/Img/GoodImg/Bmp/`:

```
# In[1]:
import os
import numpy as np
from sklearn.pipeline import Pipeline
from sklearn.svm import SVC
from sklearn.model_selection import train_test_split
from sklearn.grid_search import GridSearchCV
from sklearn.metrics import classification_report
from PIL import Image


X = []
y = []
for path, subdirs, files in os.walk('data/English/Img/GoodImg/Bmp/'):
    for filename in files:
        f = os.path.join(path, filename)
        target = filename[3:filename.index('-')]
        img = Image.open(f).convert('L').resize((30, 30),
            resample=Image.LANCZOS)
        X.append(np.array(img).reshape(900,))
        y.append(target)
X = np.array(X)
```

First we load the images and convert them to grayscale using Pillow. As with previous examples, we wrap the script in a main block to support forking additional processes during grid search. Unlike MNIST, the images of Chars74K do not have consistent dimensions, so we will resize them to 30 pixels on a side. Finally, we convert the processed image to a NumPy array:

```
In[2]:
X_train, X_test, y_train, y_test = train_test_split(X, y, test_size=.1,
random_state=11)
pipeline = Pipeline([
    ('clf', SVC(kernel='rbf', gamma=0.01, C=100))
])
parameters = {
    'clf__gamma': (0.01, 0.03, 0.1, 0.3, 1),
    'clf__C': (0.1, 0.3, 1, 3, 10, 30),
}

if __name__ == '__main__':
```

```
        grid_search = GridSearchCV(pipeline, parameters, n_jobs=3,
            verbose=1, scoring='accuracy')
        grid_search.fit(X_train, y_train)
        print('Best score: %0.3f' % grid_search.best_score_)
        print('Best parameters set:')
        best_parameters = grid_search.best_estimator_.get_params()
        for param_name in sorted(parameters.keys()):
            print('\t%s: %r' % (param_name,
                best_parameters[param_name]))
        predictions = grid_search.predict(X_test)
        print(classification_report(y_test, predictions))

    # Out[2]:
    todo
```

As with the MNIST example, we grid-search to tune the model's hyperparameters. `GridSearchCV` retrains the model using the best hyperparameter settings on all of the training data; we then evaluate this model on the test data. It is apparent that this is a more challenging task than classifying digits in MNIST; the appearances of the characters vary more widely, and the characters are perturbed more since the images were sampled from photographs rather than scanned documents. Furthermore, there are far fewer training instances for each class in Chars74K than there are in MNIST. Despite these challenges, the classifier still performs well. Its performance can be improved by adding training data, preprocessing the images differently, or using more sophisticated feature representations.

Summary

In this chapter, we discussed the SVM, a powerful model that can be used for classification and regression tasks. SVMs efficiently map features to higher dimensional spaces in which classes may be linearly separable. SVMs also maximize the margin between the decision boundary and the nearest training instances. In the next chapter, we will discuss models called ANN; like SVMs, they extend the perceptron to overcome its limitations.

12
From the Perceptron to Artificial Neural Networks

In Chapter 10, *The Perceptron* we introduced the perceptron, a linear model for binary classification. We learned that the perceptron is not a universal function approximator; its decision boundary must be a hyperplane. In Chapter 11, *From the Perceptron to Support Vector Machines* we introduced the SVM, which addresses some of the perceptron's limitations by using kernels to efficiently map the feature representations to a higher dimensional space in which the classes may be linearly separable. In this chapter, we will discuss ANNs, powerful nonlinear models for supervised and unsupervised tasks that use a different strategy to overcome the perceptron's limitations. If the perceptron is analogous to a neuron, an ANN, or **neural net**, is analogous to a brain. As billions of neurons with trillions of synapses comprise a human brain, an ANN is a directed graph of artificial neurons. The graph's edges are weighted; these weights are the parameters of the model that must be learned.

This chapter will provide an overview of the structure and training of small, feed-forward artificial neural networks. scikit-learn implements neural networks for classification, regression, and feature extraction. However, these implementations are suitable for only small networks. Training neural networks is computationally expensive; in practice, most neural networks are trained using graphics processing units with thousands of parallel processing cores. scikit-learn does not support GPUs, and it is not likely to do so in the near future. GPU acceleration is immature but rapidly developing; supporting it would add many dependencies to scikit-learn and conflict with the project's goal of being easy to install on a variety of platforms. Furthermore, other machine learning algorithms seldom require GPU acceleration to the same extent as neural nets. Training neural networks is better served by purpose-built libraries such as Caffe, TensorFlow, and Keras than general-purpose machine learning libraries such as scikit-learn.

While we will not use scikit-learn to train deep **Convolutional Neural Networks** (CNN) for object recognition or recurrent networks for speech recognition, understanding the workings of the small networks that we will train is an important prerequisite for these tasks.

Nonlinear decision boundaries

Recall from Chapter 10, *The Perceptron* that while some Boolean functions such as **AND**, **OR**, and **NAND** can be approximated by the perceptron, the linearly inseparable function **XOR** cannot, as shown in the following plots:

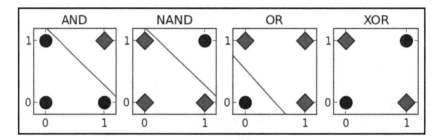

Let's review **XOR** in more detail to develop an intuition of the power of ANN. In contrast to **AND**, which outputs **1** when both of its inputs are equal to **1**, and **OR**, which outputs **1** when at least one of the inputs are equal to **1**, the output of XOR is **1** when exactly one of its inputs is equal to **1**. We can view XOR as outputting **1** when two conditions are true. The first condition is that at least one of the inputs must be equal to **1**; this is the same condition that **OR** tests. The second condition is that the inputs cannot both equal **1**; **NAND** tests this condition. We can produce the same output as **XOR** by processing the input with both **OR** and **NAND**, and then verifying that the outputs of both functions are equal to **1** using **AND**. That is, the functions **OR, NAND,** and **AND** can be composed to produce the same output as **XOR**.

A	B	A AND B	A NAND B	A OR B	A XOR B
0	0	0	1	0	0
0	1	0	1	1	1
1	0	0	1	1	1
1	1	1	0	1	0

The previous figure provides truth tables for XOR, OR, AND, and NAND for the inputs A and B. From this we can verify that inputting the output of OR and NAND to AND produces the same output as inputting A and B to XOR.

A	B	A OR B	A NAND B	(A OR B) AND (A NAND B)
0	0	0	1	0
0	1	1	1	1
1	0	1	1	1
1	1	1	0	0

Instead of trying to represent XOR with a single perceptron, we will build an ANN from multiple artificial neurons that each approximate a linear function. Each instance's feature representation will be input to two neurons; one neuron will represent NAND and the other will represent OR. The output of these neurons will be received by a third neuron that represents AND to test that both of XOR's conditions are true.

Feed-forward and feedback ANNs

ANNs are described by three components. The first is the model's **architecture**, or **topology**, which describes the types of neuron and the structure of the connections between them. Then we have the activation functions used by the artificial neurons. The third component is the learning algorithm that finds the optimal values of the weights.

There are two main types of ANN. Feed-forward neural networks are the most common type and are defined by their directed acyclic graphs. Information travels in one direction only, towards the output layer, in feed-forward neural networks. Conversely, **feedback neural networks**, or **recurrent neural networks**, contain cycles. The feedback cycles can represent an internal state for the network that can cause the network's behavior to change over time based on its input. Feed-forward neural networks are commonly used to learn a function to map an input to an output. For example, a feed-forward net can be used to recognize objects in a photo or predict the likelihood that a subscriber of a SaaS product will churn. The temporal behavior of feedback neural networks make them suitable for processing sequences of inputs. Feedback neural nets have been used to translate documents between languages and automatically transcribe speech. Because feedback neural networks are not implemented in scikit-learn, we will limit our discussion to only feed-forward neural networks.

Multi-layer perceptrons

The **multi-layer perceptron** is a simple ANN. Its name, however, is a misnomer. A multi-layer perceptron is not a single perceptron with multiple layers, but rather multiple layers of artificial neurons that resemble perceptrons. Multi-layer perceptrons have three or more layers of artificial neurons that form a directed, acyclic graph. Generally, each layer is **fully connected** to the subsequent layer; the output, or **activation**, of each artificial neuron in a layer is an input to every artificial neuron in the next layer. Features are input through the **Input layer**. The simple neurons in the input layer are connected to at least one **Hidden layer**. Hidden layers represents latent variables; these cannot be observed in the training data. The hidden neurons in these layers are often called hidden units. Finally, the last hidden layer is connected to an **Output layer**; the activations of this layer are the predicted values of the response variable. The following diagram depicts the architecture of a multi-layer perceptron with three layers. The neurons labeled **+1** are constant bias neurons and are not depicted in most architecture diagrams. This network has two input neurons, three hidden neurons, and two output neurons.

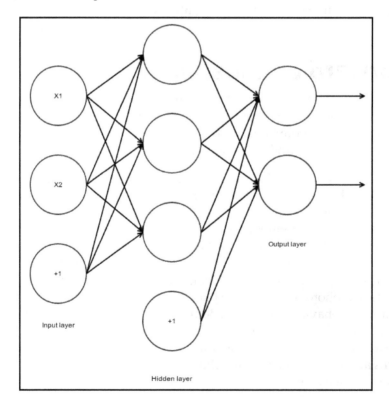

The **Input layer** is not included in the count of a network's layers, but it is counted in `MLPClassifier.n_layers_`.

Recall from `Chapter 10`, *The Perceptron* that a perceptron has one or more binary inputs, one binary output, and a Heaviside step activation function. A small change to a perceptron's weights may have no effect on its output, or it may cause its output to flip from *1* to *0* or vice versa. This will make it difficult to understand how the network's performance changes as we change its weights. For this reason, we will build our MLP from a different type of neuron. A **sigmoid neuron** has one or more real-valued inputs and one real-valued outputs, and it uses a sigmoid activation function. Plotted in the following figure, a sigmoid is a smoothed version of a step function; it approximates a step function for extreme values, but it can output any value between **0** and **1**. This allows us to understand how changes to the inputs affect the output.

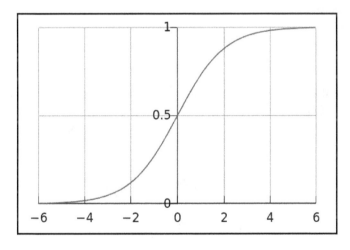

Training multi-layer perceptrons

In this section, we will discuss how to train a multi-layer perceptron. Recall from Chapter 5, *From Simple Linear Regression to Multiple Linear Regression* that we can use gradient descent to minimize a real-valued function, C, of many variables. Assume that C is a function of two variables v_1 and v_2. To understand how to change the variables to minimize C, we need a small change in the variables to produce a small change in the output. We will represent a change in the value of v_1 with Δv_1, a change in the value of v_2 with Δv_2, and a change in the value of C with ΔC. The relation between ΔC and changes to variables is given by:

$$\Delta C \approx \frac{\partial C}{\partial v_1} \Delta v_1 + \frac{\partial C}{\partial v_2} \Delta v_2$$

$\partial C / \partial v_1$ is the partial derivative of C with respect to v_1. For convenience, we will represent *$\Delta v1$* and *$\Delta v2$* as a vector:

$$\Delta v = \left(\Delta v_1, \Delta v_2 \right)^T$$

We will also represent the partial derivatives of C with respect to the variables using the gradient vector of C, ∇C :

$$\Delta C = \left(\frac{\partial C}{\partial v_1}, \frac{\partial C}{\partial v_2} \right)^T$$

We can rewrite our formula for ΔC as follows:

$$\Delta C = \nabla C \Delta v$$

On each iteration, ΔC should be negative to decrease the value of the cost function. To guarantee that ΔC will be negative, we set Δv to the following:

$$\Delta v = -\eta \nabla C$$

Here, η is a hyperparameter called the **learning rate**. We will substitute for Δv to make it clear why ΔC will be negative.

$$\Delta v = -\eta \nabla C \cdot \nabla C$$

∇C squared will always be greater than zero. We then multiply it by the learning rate and negate the product. On each iteration, we will calculate the gradient of C, ∇C, and then update the variables to take a step in the direction of the steepest decline. We've omitted one important detail for training our multi-layer perceptron: how do we understand how changes in the values of the hidden units' weights affect the cost? More concretely, how do we calculate the partial derivative of the cost function with respect to weights connecting the hidden layers?

Backpropagation

We learned that gradient descent iteratively minimizes a function by calculating its gradient and using the gradient to update the function's parameters. To minimize the cost function of our multi-layer perceptron, we need to be able to calculate its gradient. Recall that multi-layer perceptrons contain layers of units that represent latent variables. We cannot use a cost function to calculate their errors; the training data indicates the desired output of the entire network, but it does not describe how the hidden units should behave. Since we cannot calculate the hidden units' errors, we cannot calculate their gradients or update their weights. A naive solution to this problem is to randomly change the weights for the hidden units. If a random change to one of the weights decreases the value of the cost function, the weight is updated and another change is evaluated. The computational cost of this solution is prohibitive for even trivial networks. In this section, we will describe a more efficient solution; we will calculate the gradient of a neural network's cost function with respect to its weights using the backpropagation algorithm, or backprop. Backpropagation allows us to understand how each weight contributes to the error, and therefore how to update the weights to minimize the cost function.

The algorithm's name is a portmanteau of backward propagation, and refers to the direction in which errors flow through the layers of the network when calculating the gradients. Backprop is commonly used in conjunction with an optimization algorithm like gradient descent to train feed-forward neural networks. It can be theoretically be used to train a feed-forward network with any number of hidden units arranged in any number of layers.

Like gradient descent, backprop is an iterative algorithm. Each iteration consists of two phases. The first phase is forward propagation, or the forward pass. In the forward pass, inputs are propagated through the network's layers of neurons until they reach the output layer. The loss function can then be used to calculate the error of the prediction. The second phase is backward propagation. Errors are propagated backward from the cost function towards the inputs so that each neuron's contribution to the error can be approximated. This process is based on the chain rule, which can be used to calculate the derivative of the composition of two or more functions. We demonstrated earlier that neural networks can compose linear functions together to approximate complex, nonlinear functions. These errors can then be used to calculate the gradients that gradient descent requires to update the weights. After the weights have been updated, features can be propagated forward through the network again to begin the next iteration.

The chain rule can be used to calculate the derivative of the composition of two or more functions. Assume that variable z depends on y, and that y depends on x. The derivative of z with respect to x is given by: $\frac{dz}{dx} = \frac{dz}{dy} \cdot \frac{dy}{dx}$

To propagate forward through a network, we calculate the activations of the neurons in a layer, and input the activations to the connected neurons in the next layer. To do so, we must first calculate the preactivation of each neuron in the layer. Recall that the preactivation of a neuron is the linear combination of its inputs and its weights. Next, we calculate the activation of each neuron by applying its activation function to its preactivation. The activations of this layer are then input to the next layer in the network.

To propagate backward through the network, we first calculate the partial derivative of the cost function with respect to the activations of the last hidden layer. We can then calculate the partial derivative of the last hidden layer's activations with respect to its preactivations. Next, we calculate the partial derivative of the last hidden layer's preactivations with respect to its weights, and so on until we have reached the input layer. Through this process, we approximate each neuron's contribution to the error, and we calculate the gradients necessary to update their weights and minimize the cost function. More concretely, for each unit in each layer, we must calculate two partial derivatives. The first is the derivative of the error with respect to the activation of the unit. This derivative is not used to update the unit's weights; instead, it is used to update the weights of the units connected to it in the preceding layer. Second, we will calculate the partial derivative of the error with respect to the unit's weights in order to update their values and minimize the cost function. Let's work through an example. We will train a neural network with two input units, one hidden layer with two hidden units, and one output unit, as visualized here:

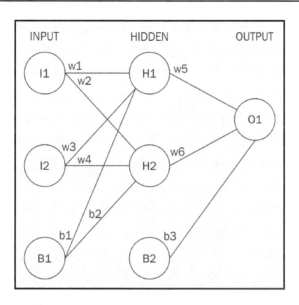

Let's assume that the weights were initialized to the values in the following table:

Weight	Value
w_1	.4
w_2	.3
w_3	.8
w_4	.1
w_5	.6
w_6	.2
b_1	.5
b_2	.2
b_3	.9

The feature vector is *[0.8, 0.3]*, and the true value of the response variable is *0.5*. Let's calculate the first forward pass, starting with hidden unit h_1. First we will calculate the preactivation of h_1. Then we will apply the logistic sigmoid function to the preactivation to calculate the activation.

$$pre_{h_1} = w_1 i_1 + w_3 i_2 + b_1$$

$$pre_{h_1} = 0.4 \times 0.8 + 0.8 \times 0.3 + 0.5 = 1.06$$

$$act_{h_1} = \frac{1}{1 - e^{-h1_{pre}}} = 0.743$$

We can use the same process to calculate the activation of h_2, which is *0.615*. We then input the activations of hidden units h_1 and h_2 to the output layer and similarly calculate the activation of o_1, *0.813*. We can now calculate the error of the network's prediction. For this network, we will use the squared error cost function, which is given by the following formula:

$$E = \frac{1}{2} \sum_{i=1}^{n} (y_i - \hat{y}_i)^2$$

Here, n is the number of output units, $\hat{y}_i$ is the activation of output neuron o_i, and y_i is the true value of the response variable. Our network has a single output unit, so n is *1*. The network predicted *0.813*; the true value of the response variable is *0.5*, so the error is *0.313*. Now we can work through updating the weight w_5. We must first calculate ∂E/∂w_5, or how much changing w_5 affects the error. By the chain rule, ∂E/∂w_5 is equal to:

$$\frac{\partial E}{\partial w_5} = \frac{\partial E}{\partial act_{o_1}} \cdot \frac{\partial act_{o_1}}{\partial pre_{o_1}} \cdot \frac{\partial pre_{o_1}}{\partial w_5}$$

That is, we can approximate how much the error changes with respect to w_5 by answering the following:

- How much does a change in the activation of o_1 affect the error?
- How much does a change in the preactivation of o_1 affect the activation of o_1?
- How much does a change in the weight w_5 affect the preactivation of o_1?

We will then subtract the product of $\partial E/\partial w_5$ and our learning rate from the value of w_5 to update it. Let's answer the first question by approximating how the error changes with respect to the activation of 0_1. The partial derivative of the cost function with respect to the activation of the output unit is given by:

$$\frac{\partial E}{\partial act_{o_1}} = -\left(y_1 - act_{o_1}\right)$$

$$\frac{\partial E}{\partial act_{o_1}} = -\left(0.5 - 0.813\right) = 0.313$$

Next we will answer the second question by approximating how the activation of 0_1 changes with respect to its preactivation. The derivative of the logistic function is given by the following:

$$\frac{d}{dx} f(x) = f(x)\left(1 - f(x)\right)$$

Here, $f(x)$ is the logistic function, $1/(1 + e^x)$.

$$\frac{\partial act_{o_1}}{\partial pre_{0_1}} = act_{0_1}\left(1 - act_{o_1}\right)$$

$$\frac{\partial act_{o_1}}{\partial pre_{0_1}} = 0.813 \times \left(1 - 813\right) = 0.152$$

Finally, we will approximate how the preactivation of o_1 changes with respect to w_5. Recall that the preactivation is the linear combination of the weights and inputs.

$$pre_{o_1} = w_5 act_{h_1} + w_6 act_{h_2} + b_2$$

$$\frac{\partial pre_{o_1}}{\partial w_5} = 1 \times act_{h_1} \times w_5^0 + 0 + 0 = act_{h_1} = 0.743$$

The derivatives of both the bias term b_2 and $w_6 act_{h2}$ are 0. Both terms are constant with respect to w_5; changes to w_5 do not affect $w_6 act_{h2}$.

Now that we have answered our three questions, we can calculate the partial derivative of the error with respect to w_5, as follows:

$$\frac{\partial E}{\partial w_5} = 0.313 \times 0.152 \times 0.743 = 0.035$$

We can now update the value of w_5 by subtracting from it the product of our learning rate and $\partial E/\partial w_5$. We can then follow a similar process to update the remaining weights. This completes the first backward pass; we can now forward-propagate through the network again using the updated weights.

Training a multi-layer perceptron to approximate XOR

Let's use scikit-learn to train a network that approximates XOR. We pass the `activation='logistic'` keyword argument to the `MLPClassifier` constructor to specify that the neurons should use the logistic sigmoid activation function. The `hidden_layer_sizes` parameter takes a tuple of integers that indicate the number of hidden units in each hidden layer. We will train a network with the same architecture as the network we used in the previous section; it has one hidden layer with two hidden units and an output layer with one output unit:

```
# In[1]:
from sklearn.model_selection import train_test_split
from sklearn.neural_network import MLPClassifier

y = [0, 1, 1, 0]
```

```
X = [[0, 0], [0, 1], [1, 0], [1, 1]]

clf = MLPClassifier(solver='lbfgs', activation='logistic',
  hidden_layer_sizes=(2,), random_state=20)
clf.fit(X, y)

predictions = clf.predict(X)
print('Accuracy: %s' % clf.score(X, y))
for i, p in enumerate(predictions):
    print('True: %s, Predicted: %s' % (y[i], p))

# Out[1]:
Accuracy: 1.0
True: 0, Predicted: 0
True: 1, Predicted: 1
True: 1, Predicted: 1
True: 0, Predicted: 0
```

After a few iterations, the network converges. Let's inspect the weights that were learned and complete a forward pass for the feature vector *[1, 1]*:

```
# In[2]:
print('Weights connecting the input layer and the hidden layer: \n%s' %
clf.coefs_[0])
print('Hidden layer bias weights: \n%s' % clf.intercepts_[0])
print('Weights connecting the hidden layer and the output layer:
  \n%s' % clf.coefs_[1])
print('Output layer bias weight: \n%s' % clf.intercepts_[1])

# Out[2]:
Weights connecting the input layer and the hidden layer:
[[ 6.11803955  6.35656369]
 [ 5.79147859  6.14551916]]
Hidden layer bias weights:
[-9.38637909 -2.77751771]
Weights connecting the hidden layer and the output layer:
[[-14.95481734]
 [ 14.53080968]]
Output layer bias weight:
[-7.2284531]
```

To forward-propagate, we must calculate the following:

$$pre_{h_1} = b_1 + w_1 i_1 + w_3 i_2$$

$$act_{h_1} = \frac{1}{1 - e^{-pre_{h_1}}}$$

$$pre_{h_2} = b_2 + w_2 i_1 + w_4 i_2$$

$$act_{h_2} = \frac{1}{1 - e^{-pre_{h_2}}}$$

$$pre_{o_1} = b_3 + w_5 act_{h_1} + w_6 act_{h_2}$$

$$act_{o_1} = \frac{1}{1 - e^{-pre_{o_1}}}$$

$$pre_{h_1} = -9.38637909 + 6.11803955 \times 1 + 5.79147859 \times 1 = 3.088$$

$$act_{h_1} = \frac{1}{1 + e^{-3.088}} = 0.956$$

$$pre_{h_2} = -2.77751771 + 6.3565639 \times 1 + 6.14551916 \times 1 = 9.159$$

$$act_{h_2} = \frac{1}{1 + e^{-9.159}} = 1.000$$

$$pre_{o_1} = -7.2284531 + -14.95481734 \times 1 + 14.53080968 \times 1 = -7.002$$

$$act_{o_1} = \frac{1}{1 + e^{-pre_{-7.002}}} = 0.001$$

The probability that the response variable is the positive class is *0.001*; the network predicts $1 \oplus 1 = 0$.

Training a multi-layer perceptron to classify handwritten digits

In the previous chapter, we used a SVM to classify the handwritten digits in the MNIST dataset. In this section, we will classify the images using an ANN:

```
# In[1]:
from sklearn.datasets import load_digits
from sklearn.model_selection import cross_val_score
from sklearn.pipeline import Pipeline
from sklearn.preprocessing import StandardScaler
from sklearn.neural_network.multilayer_perceptron import
  MLPClassifier

if __name__ == '__main__':
    digits = load_digits()
    X = digits.data
    y = digits.target
    pipeline = Pipeline([
        ('ss', StandardScaler()),
        ('mlp', MLPClassifier(hidden_layer_sizes=(150, 100),
          alpha=0.1, max_iter=300, random_state=20))
    ])
    print(cross_val_score(pipeline, X, y, n_jobs=-1))

# Out[1]:
[ 0.94850498  0.94991653  0.90771812]
```

First we use the `load_digits` convenience function to load the MNIST dataset. We will fork additional processes during cross validation, which requires execution from a main-protected block. Scaling the features is particularly important for ANNs, and will help some learning algorithms to converge more quickly. Next, we create a `Pipeline` that scales the data before fitting an `MLPClassifier`. This network contains an input layer, a hidden layer with `150` units, a second hidden layer with `100` units, and an output layer. We also increased the value of the regularization hyperparameter, `alpha`, and increased the maximum number of iterations from the default of `200` to `300`. Finally, we print the accuracies of the three cross validation folds. The mean accuracy is comparable to the accuracy of the support vector classifier. Adding more hidden units or hidden layers and grid searching to tune the hyperparameters can further improve the accuracy.

Summary

In this chapter, we introduced ANN, powerful models for classification and regression that can represent complex functions by composing several artificial neurons. In particular, we discussed directed acyclic graphs of artificial neurons called feed-forward neural networks. Multi-layer perceptrons are a type of feed-forward network in which each layer is fully connected to the subsequent layer. An MLP with one hidden layer and a finite number of hidden units is a universal function approximator; it can represent any continuous function, though it will not necessarily be able to learn appropriate weights automatically. We described how the hidden layers of a network represent latent variables and how their weights can be learned using the backpropagation algorithm. Finally, we used scikit-learn's multi-layer perceptron implementation to approximate the function XOR and to classify handwritten digits.

13
K-means

In previous chapters, we discussed supervised learning tasks; we examined algorithms for regression and classification that learned from labeled training data. In this chapter, we will introduce our first unsupervised learning task: clustering. Clustering is used to find groups of similar observations within a set of unlabeled data. We will discuss the K-means clustering algorithm, apply it to an image compression problem, and learn to measure its performance. Finally, we will work through a semi-supervised learning problem that combines clustering with classification.

Clustering

Recall from Chapter 1, *The Fundamentals of Machine Learning* that the goal of unsupervised learning is to discover hidden structures or patterns in unlabeled training data. **Clustering**, or **cluster analysis**, is the task of grouping observations so that members of the same group, or **cluster**, are more similar to each other by some metric than they are to members of other clusters. As with supervised learning, we will represent an observation as an n-dimensional vector.

For example, assume that your training data consists of the samples plotted in the following figure:

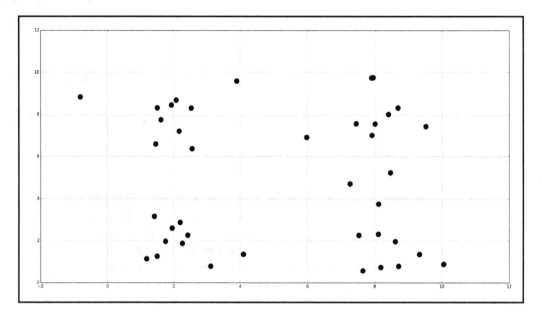

Clustering might produce the following two groups, indicated by squares and circles:

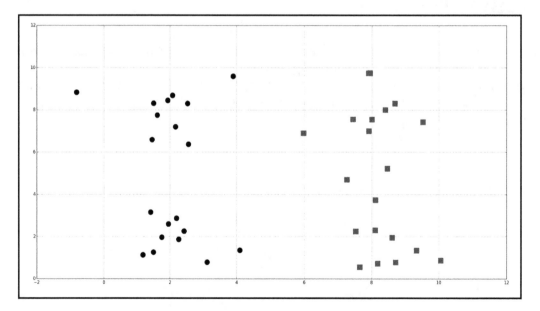

Clustering can also produce the following four groups:

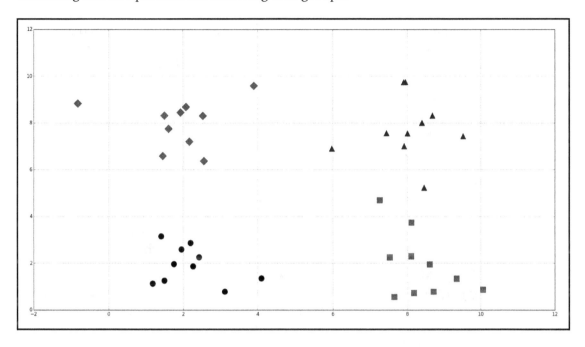

Clustering is commonly used to explore a dataset. Social networks can be clustered to identify communities and to suggest missing connections between people. In biology, clustering is used to find groups of genes with similar expression patterns. Recommendation systems sometimes employ clustering to identify products or media that might appeal to a user. In marketing, clustering is used to find segments of similar consumers. In the following sections, we will work through an example of using the K-means algorithm to cluster a dataset.

K-means

The K-means algorithm is a clustering method that is popular because of its speed and scalability. K-means is an iterative process of moving the centers of the clusters, called the **centroids**, to the mean position of their constituent instances and re-assigning instances to the clusters with the closest centroids. The titular k is a hyperparameter that specifies the number of clusters that should be created; K-means automatically assigns observations to clusters but cannot determine the appropriate number of clusters. k must be a positive integer that is less than the number of instances in the training set. Sometimes the number of clusters is specified by the clustering problem's context. For example, a company that manufactures shoes might know that it is able to support manufacturing three new models. To understand what groups of customers to target with each model, it surveys customers and creates three clusters from the results, that is, the number of clusters specified by the problem's context. Other problems may not require a specific number of clusters, and the optimal number of clusters may be ambiguous. We will discuss a heuristic for estimating the optimal number of clusters called the **elbow method** later in this chapter.

The parameters of K-means are the positions of the clusters' centroids and the observations that are assigned to each cluster. Like generalized linear models and decision trees, the optimal values of K-means' parameters are found by minimizing a cost function. The cost function for K-means is given by the following equation:

$$J = \sum_{k=1}^{K} \sum_{i \in C_k} ||x_i - \mu_k||^2$$

Here, μ_k is the centroid for cluster k. The cost function sums the distortions of the clusters. Each cluster's distortion is equal to the sum of the squared distances between its centroid and its constituent instances. The distortion is small for compact clusters and large for clusters that contain scattered instances. The parameters that minimize the cost function are learned through an iterative process of assigning observations to clusters and then moving the clusters. First, the clusters' centroids are initialized, often by randomly selecting instances. During each iteration, K-means assigns observations to the cluster that they are closest to and then moves the centroids to their assigned observations' mean location. Let's work through an example by hand using the training data shown in the following table:

Instance	x0	x1
1	7	5
2	5	7

3	7	7
4	3	3
5	4	6
6	1	4
7	0	0
8	2	2
9	8	7
10	6	8
11	5	5
12	3	7

There are two explanatory variables; one feature is extracted from each variable. The instances are plotted in the following figure:

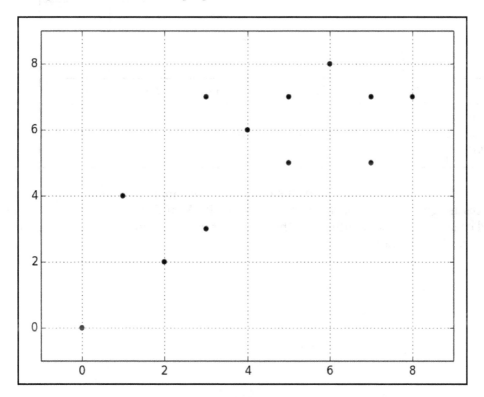

Assume that K-means initializes the centroid for the first cluster to the fifth instance and the centroid for the second cluster to the eleventh instance. For each instance, we will calculate its distance from both centroids and assign it to the cluster with the closest centroid. The initial assignments are shown in the *Cluster* column of the following table:

Instance	x0	x1	C1 distance	C2 distance	Last cluster	Cluster	Changed?
1	7	5	3.16228	2	None	C2	Yes
2	5	7	1.41421	2	None	C1	Yes
3	7	7	3.16228	2.82843	None	C2	Yes
4	3	3	3.16228	2.82843	None	C2	Yes
5	4	6	0	1.41421	None	C1	Yes
6	1	4	3.60555	4.12311	None	C1	Yes
7	0	0	7.21110	7.07107	None	C2	Yes
8	2	2	4.47214	4.24264	None	C2	Yes
9	8	7	4.12311	3.60555	None	C2	Yes
10	6	8	2.82843	3.16228	None	C1	Yes
11	5	5	1.41421	0	None	C2	Yes
12	3	7	1.41421	2.82843	None	C1	Yes
C1 centroid	4	6					
C2 centroid	5	5					

The plotted centroids and the initial cluster assignments are shown in the following graph. Instances assigned to the first cluster are marked with **X**, and instances assigned to the second cluster are marked with dots. The markers for the centroids are larger than the markers for the instances.

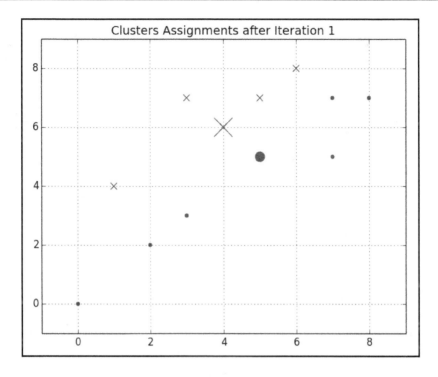

Clusters Assignments after Iteration 1

Now, we will move both centroids to the means of their constituent instances, recalculate the distances of the training instances to the centroids, and reassign the instances to the closest centroids. The new clusters are plotted in the following graph. Note that the centroids are diverging and several instances have changed their assignments.

Instance	x0	x1	C1 distance	C2 distance	Last cluster	New cluster	Changed?
1	7	5	3.492850	2.575394	C2	C2	No
2	5	7	1.341641	2.889107	C1	C1	No
3	7	7	3.255764	3.749830	C2	C1	Yes
4	3	3	3.492850	1.943067	C2	C2	No
5	4	6	0.447214	1.943067	C1	C1	No
6	1	4	3.687818	3.574285	C1	C2	Yes
7	0	0	7.443118	6.169378	C2	C2	No
8	2	2	4.753946	3.347250	C2	C2	No

9	8	7	4.242641	4.463000	C2	C1	Yes
10	6	8	2.720294	4.113194	C1	C1	No
11	5	5	1.843909	0.958315	C2	C2	No
12	3	7	1	3.260775	C1	C1	No
C1 centroid	3.8	6.4					
C2 centroid	4.571429	4.142857					

The following plot visualizes the centroids and cluster assignments after the second iteration:

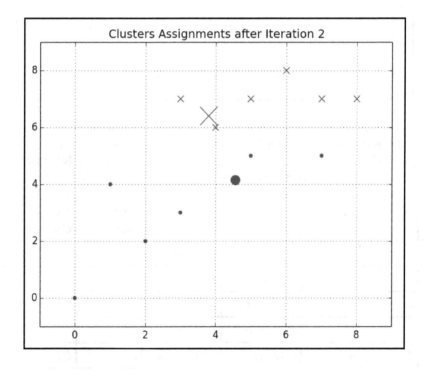

Now we will move the centroids to the means of their constituents' locations again and reassign the instances to their nearest centroids. The centroids continue to diverge, as shown in this figure:

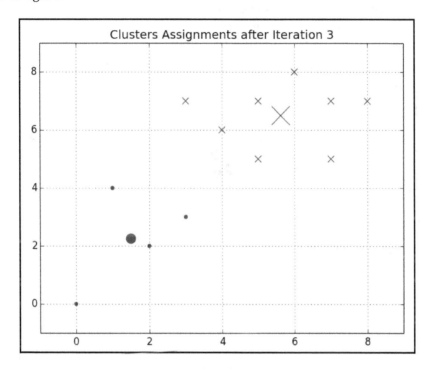

None of the instances' centroid assignments will change in the next iteration; k-means will continue iterating until some stopping criteria is satisfied. Usually, this criteria is either a threshold for the difference between the values of the cost function for subsequent iterations, or a threshold for the change in the positions of the centroids between subsequent iterations. If these stopping criteria are small enough, k-means will converge on an optimum. However, the time required to converge increases as the value of the stopping criteria decreases. Furthermore, it is important to note that K-means will not necessarily converge on the global optimum regardless of the values of the stopping criteria.

Local optima

Recall that K-means often initializes the centroids to the positions of randomly selected observations. Sometimes, this random initialization is unlucky and the centroids are set to positions that cause K-means to converge to a local optimum. For example, assume that K-means randomly initializes two cluster centroids to the following positions:

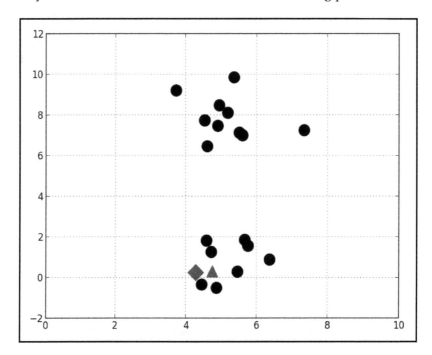

K-means will eventually converge on a local optimum, like what is shown in the preceding figure. These clusters may be informative, but it is more likely that the top and bottom groups of observations are more informative clusters. Some local optima are better than others. To avoid unlucky initialization, K-means is often repeated dozens or hundreds of times. In each iteration, it is randomly initialized to different starting cluster positions. The initialization that minimizes the cost function best is selected.

Selecting K with the elbow method

If *k* is not specified by the problem's context, the optimal number of clusters can be estimated using a technique called the elbow method. The elbow method plots the value of the cost function produced by different values of *k*. As *k* increases, the average distortion will decrease; each cluster will have fewer constituent instances, and the instances will be closer to their respective centroids. However, the improvements to the average dispersion will decline as *k* increases. The value of *k* at which the improvement to the dispersion declines the most is called the elbow. Let's use the elbow method to choose the number of clusters for a dataset. The following scatter plot visualizes a dataset with two obvious clusters:

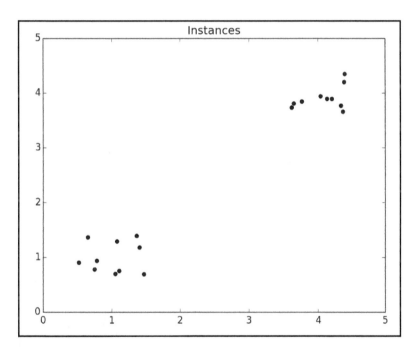

We will calculate and plot the mean dispersion of the clusters for each value of k from 1 to 10 with this code:

```
# In[1]:
import numpy as np
from sklearn.cluster import KMeans
from scipy.spatial.distance import cdist
import matplotlib.pyplot as plt

c1x = np.random.uniform(0.5, 1.5, (1, 10))
c1y = np.random.uniform(0.5, 1.5, (1, 10))
```

```
c2x = np.random.uniform(3.5, 4.5, (1, 10))
c2y = np.random.uniform(3.5, 4.5, (1, 10))
x = np.hstack((c1x, c2x))
y = np.hstack((c1y, c2y))
X = np.vstack((x, y)).T

K = range(1, 10)
meanDispersions = []
for k in K:
    kmeans = KMeans(n_clusters=k)
    kmeans.fit(X)
    meanDispersions.append(sum(np.min(cdist(X,
        kmeans.cluster_centers_, 'euclidean'), axis=1)) / X.shape[0])

plt.plot(K, meanDispersions, 'bx-')
plt.xlabel('k')
plt.ylabel('Average Dispersion')
plt.title('Selecting k with the Elbow Method')
plt.show()
```

The script produces the following plot.

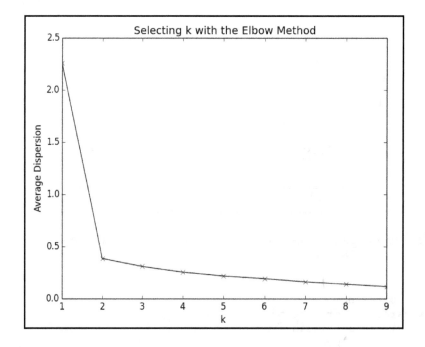

The average dispersion improves rapidly as we increase *k* from *1* to *2*. There is little improvement for values of *k* greater than *2*. Now let's use the elbow method on the following dataset with three clusters:

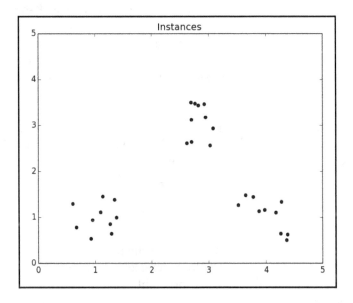

The following is the elbow plot for the dataset. From this we can see that the rate of improvement to the average distortion declines the most when adding a fourth cluster. That is, the elbow method confirms that *k* should be set to *3* for this dataset.

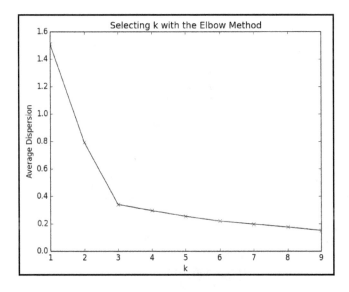

Evaluating clusters

We defined machine learning as the design and study of systems that learn from experience to improve their performance of a task as measured by some metric. K-means is an unsupervised learning algorithm; there are no labels or ground truth to compare with the clusters. However, we can still evaluate the performance of the algorithm using intrinsic measures. We have already discussed measuring the distortions of clusters. In this section, we will discuss another performance measure for clustering called **silhouette coefficient**. The silhouette coefficient is a measure of compactness and separation of clusters. It increases as the quality of clusters increases; it is large for compact clusters that are far from each other and small for large, overlapping clusters. The silhouette coefficient is calculated per instance; for a set of instances, it is calculated as the mean of the individual samples' scores. The silhouette coefficient for an instance is calculated with the following equation:

$$s = \frac{ba}{max(a, b)}$$

a is the mean distance between the instances in the cluster. *b* is the mean distance between the instance and the instances in the next closest cluster. The following example runs K-means four times to create two, three, four, and eight clusters from a toy dataset, and calculates the silhouette coefficient for each run:

```
# In[1]:
import numpy as np
from sklearn.cluster import KMeans
from sklearn import metrics
import matplotlib.pyplot as plt

plt.subplot(3, 2, 1)
x1 = np.array([1, 2, 3, 1, 5, 6, 5, 5, 6, 7, 8, 9, 7, 9])
x2 = np.array([1, 3, 2, 2, 8, 6, 7, 6, 7, 1, 2, 1, 1, 3])
X = np.array(zip(x1, x2)).reshape(len(x1), 2)

plt.xlim([0, 10])
plt.ylim([0, 10])
plt.title('Instances')
plt.scatter(x1, x2)
colors = ['b', 'g', 'r', 'c', 'm', 'y', 'k', 'b']
markers = ['o', 's', 'D', 'v', '^', 'p', '*', '+']
tests = [2, 3, 4, 5, 8]
subplot_counter = 1
for t in tests:
    subplot_counter += 1
    plt.subplot(3, 2, subplot_counter)
```

```
kmeans_model = KMeans(n_clusters=t).fit(X)
for i, l in enumerate(kmeans_model.labels_):
    plt.plot(x1[i], x2[i], color=colors[l], marker=markers[l],
        ls='None')
plt.xlim([0, 10])
plt.ylim([0, 10])
plt.title('K = %s, Silhouette Coefficient = %.03f' % (t,
    metrics.silhouette_score(X, kmeans_model.labels_,
    metric='euclidean')))
plt.show()
```

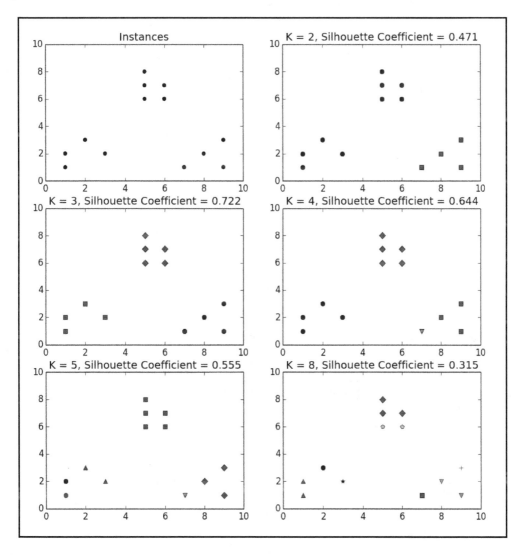

The dataset contains three obvious clusters. Accordingly, the silhouette coefficient is greatest when **K** is equal to **3**. Setting **K** equal to **8** produces clusters of instances that are as close to each other as they are to the instances in some of the other clusters, and the silhouette coefficient of these clusters is smallest.

Image quantization

In previous sections, we used clustering to explore the structure of a dataset. Now let's apply it to a different problem. **Image quantization** is a lossy compression method that replaces a range of similar colors in an image with a single color. Quantization reduces the size of the image file since fewer bits are required to represent the colors. In the following example, we will use clustering to discover a compressed palette for an image that contains its most important colors. We will then rebuild the image using the compressed palette. First we read and flatten the image:

```
# In[1]:
import numpy as np
import matplotlib.pyplot as plt
from sklearn.cluster import KMeans
from sklearn.utils import shuffle
from PIL import Image

original_img = np.array(Image.open('tree.jpg'), dtype=np.float64) /
    255
original_dimensions = tuple(original_img.shape)
width, height, depth = tuple(original_img.shape)
image_flattened = np.reshape(original_img, (width * height, depth))
```

We then use K-means to create 64 clusters from a sample of 1000 randomly selected colors. Each of the clusters will be a color in the compressed palette:

```
# In[2]:
image_array_sample = shuffle(image_flattened, random_state=0)[:1000]
estimator = KMeans(n_clusters=64, random_state=0)
estimator.fit(image_array_sample)

# Out[2]:
KMeans(algorithm='auto', copy_x=True, init='k-means++',
 max_iter=300,
    n_clusters=64, n_init=10, n_jobs=1, precompute_distances='auto',
    random_state=0, tol=0.0001, verbose=0)
```

Next, we predict the cluster assignment for each of the pixels in the original image:

```
# In[3]:
cluster_assignments = estimator.predict(image_flattened)
```

Finally, we create the compressed image from the compressed palette and cluster assignments:

```
# In[4]:
compressed_palette = estimator.cluster_centers_
compressed_img = np.zeros((width, height, compressed_palette.shape[1]))
label_idx = 0
for i in range(width):
    for j in range(height):
        compressed_img[i][j] =
            compressed_palette[cluster_assignments[label_idx]]
        label_idx += 1

plt.subplot(121)
plt.title('Original Image', fontsize=24)
plt.imshow(original_img)
plt.axis('off')
plt.subplot(122)
plt.title('Compressed Image', fontsize=24)
plt.imshow(compressed_img)
plt.axis('off')
plt.show()
```

The original and compressed versions of the image are shown in the following figure:

Clustering to learn features

In this example, we will combine clustering with classification in a semi-supervised learning problem. We will learn features by clustering unlabeled data, and use the learned features to build a supervised classifier.

Suppose that you own a cat and a dog. Further suppose that you have purchased a smartphone, ostensibly to use to communicate with humans, but in practice just to use to photograph your cat and dog. Your photographs are awesome, and you are certain that your friends and co-workers would love to review all of them in detail. You'd like to be courteous and respect that some people will only want to see your cat photos while others will only want to see your dog photos, but separating the photos is laborious. Let's build a semi-supervised learning system that can classify images of cats and dogs.

Recall from `Chapter 3`, *Classification and Regression with K-Nearest Neighbors* that a naive approach to classifying images is to use the intensities, or brightnesses, of all the pixels as features. This approach produces high-dimensional feature vectors for even small images. Unlike the high-dimensional feature vectors we used to represent documents, these vectors are not sparse. Furthermore, it is obvious that this approach is sensitive to the image's illumination, scale, and orientation. We will extract **SURF descriptors** from the images and cluster them to learn a feature representation. SURF descriptors describe interesting regions of an image and are somewhat invariant to scale, rotation, and illumination. We will then represent an image with a vector with one element for each cluster of descriptors. Each element will encode the number of descriptors extracted from the image that were assigned to the cluster. This approach is sometimes called the **bag-of-features** representation, as the collection of clusters is analogous to the bag-of-words representation's vocabulary. We will use *1,000* images of cats and *1,000* images of dogs from the training set for Kaggle's Dogs vs. Cats competition. The dataset can be downloaded from `https://www.kaggle.com/c/dogs-vs-cats/data`. We will label cats as the positive class and dogs as the negative class. Note that the images have different dimensions; since our feature vectors do not represent pixels, we do not need to resize the images to have the same dimensions. We will train using the first *60%* of the images and test on the remaining *40%*:

```
# In[1]:
import numpy as np
import mahotas as mh
from mahotas.features import surf
from sklearn.linear_model import LogisticRegression
from sklearn.metrics import *
from sklearn.cluster import MiniBatchKMeans
import glob
```

First, we load the images, convert them to grayscale, and extract SURF descriptors. SURF descriptors can be extracted more quickly than many similar features, but extracting descriptors from *2,000* images is still computationally expensive. Unlike previous examples, this script requires several minutes to execute on most computers:

```
# In[2]:
all_instance_filenames = []
all_instance_targets = []

for f in glob.glob('cats-and-dogs-img/*.jpg'):
    target = 1 if 'cat' in os.path.split(f)[1] else 0
    all_instance_filenames.append(f)
    all_instance_targets.append(target)

surf_features = []
for f in all_instance_filenames:
    image = mh.imread(f, as_grey=True)
    # The first 6 elements of each descriptor describe its position
        and orientation.
    # We require only the descriptor.
    surf_features.append(surf.surf(image)[:, 5:])

train_len = int(len(all_instance_filenames) * .60)
X_train_surf_features = np.concatenate(surf_features[:train_len])
X_test_surf_feautres = np.concatenate(surf_features[train_len:])
y_train = all_instance_targets[:train_len]
y_test = all_instance_targets[train_len:]
```

We then group the extracted descriptors into 300 clusters. We use `MiniBatchKMeans`, a variation of K-means that uses a random sample of the instances in each iteration. Because it computes the distances to the centroids for only a sample of the instances in each iteration, `MiniBatchKMeans` converges more quickly, but its clusters' distortions may be greater. In practice, the results are similar, and this compromise is acceptable:

```
# In[3]:
n_clusters = 300
estimator = MiniBatchKMeans(n_clusters=n_clusters)
estimator.fit_transform(X_train_surf_features)

# Out[3]:
array([[ 0.6056733 ,  2.70938102,  1.22470857, ...,  0.40240388,
         1.36376676,  0.91444056],
       [ 1.17256268,  2.15959095,  1.80512123, ...,  1.25544983,
         2.14938607,  0.92937648],
       [ 4.05884662,  1.87604644,  5.28951557, ...,  4.32944494,
         5.41296044,  3.89081466],
       ...,
```

```
[ 0.6193189 ,  2.92864247,  1.1535589 , ...,  0.36941273,
  1.18161751,  1.09170526],
[ 1.68619226,  3.95702531,  0.93771461, ...,  1.37208184,
  0.80844426,  2.08232525],
[ 1.09366926,  1.87174791,  1.99117652, ...,  1.12510896,
  2.15558684,  1.0511277 ]])
```

Next, we construct feature vectors for the training and testing data. We find the cluster associated with each of the extracted SURF descriptors and count them using NumPy's `binCount` function. This results in a 300-dimensional feature vector for each instance:

```
# In[4]:
X_train = []
for instance in surf_features[:train_len]:
    clusters = estimator.predict(instance)
    features = np.bincount(clusters)
    if len(features) < n_clusters:
        features = np.append(features, np.zeros((1, n_clusters-
            len(features))))
    X_train.append(features)

X_test = []
for instance in surf_features[train_len:]:
    clusters = estimator.predict(instance)
    features = np.bincount(clusters)
    if len(features) < n_clusters:
        features = np.append(features, np.zeros((1, n_clusters-
            len(features))))
    X_test.append(features)
```

Finally, we train a logistic regression classifier on the feature vectors and targets, and assess its precision, recall, and accuracy:

```
# In[5]:
clf = LogisticRegression(C=0.001, penalty='l2')
clf.fit(X_train, y_train)
predictions = clf.predict(X_test)
print(classification_report(y_test, predictions))

# Out[5]:
             precision    recall   f1-score    support

          0       0.69      0.77       0.73        378
          1       0.77      0.69       0.72        420

avg / total       0.73      0.72       0.72        798
```

Summary

In this chapter, we discussed our first unsupervised learning task, clustering. Clustering is used to discover structures in unlabeled data. We learned about the K-means clustering algorithm, which iteratively assigns instances to clusters and refines the positions of the cluster centroids. While K-means learns from experience without supervision, its performance is still measurable; we learned to use distortion and the silhouette coefficient to evaluate clusters. We applied K-means to two different problems. First, we used K-means for image quantizationK a compression technique that represents a range of colors with a single color. We also used K-means to learn features in a semi-supervised image classification problem.

In the next chapter we will discuss another unsupervised learning task called dimensionality reduction. Like the semi-supervised feature representations we created to classify images of cats and dogs, dimensionality reduction can be used to reduce the dimensions of a feature representation while retaining as much information as possible.

14
Dimensionality Reduction with Principal Component Analysis

In this chapter, we will discuss a technique for reducing the dimensions of data called **principal component analysis** (**PCA**). Dimensionality reduction is motivated by several problems. Firstly, it can be used to mitigate problems caused by the curse of dimensionality. Secondly, dimensionality reduction can be used to compress data while minimizing the amount of information that is lost. Thirdly, understanding the structure of data with hundreds of dimensions can be difficult; data with only two or three dimensions can be visualized easily. We will use PCA to visualize a high-dimensional dataset in two dimensions and to build a face recognition system.

Principal component analysis

Recall from previous chapters that problems involving high-dimensional data can be affected by the curse of dimensionality. As the number of dimensions of a dataset increases, the number of samples required for an estimator to generalize increases exponentially. Acquiring such large data may be infeasible in some applications, and learning from large datasets requires more memory and processing power. Furthermore, the sparseness of data often increases with its dimensions. It can become more difficult to detect similar instances in high-dimensional space as all instances are similarly sparse.

PCA also known as the **Karhunen-Loeve Transform (KLT)**, is a technique for finding patterns in high-dimensional data. PCA is commonly used to explore and visualize high-dimensional datasets. It can also be used to compress data and to process data before it is used by another estimator. PCA reduces a set of possibly correlated high-dimensional variables to a lower dimensional set of linearly uncorrelated synthetic variables called **principal components**. The lower dimensional data preserves as much of the variance of the original data as possible. PCA reduces the dimensions of a dataset by projecting the data onto a lower dimensional subspace. For example, a two-dimensional dataset could be reduced by projecting the points onto a line; each instance in the dataset would then be represented by a single value rather than by a pair of values. A three-dimensional dataset could be reduced to two dimensions by projecting the variables onto a plane. In general, an m-dimensional dataset can be reduced by projecting onto an n-dimensional subspace, where n is less than m. More formally, PCA can be used to find a set of vectors that span a subspace that minimizes the sum of the squared errors of the projected data. This projection will retain the greatest proportion of the original dataset's variance.

Imagine that you are a photographer for a gardening supply catalog, and you are tasked with photographing a watering can. The watering can is three-dimensional, but the photograph is two-dimensional; you must create a two-dimensional representation that describes as much of the watering can as possible. The following are four pictures that you can use:

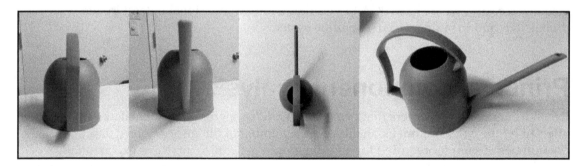

In the first photograph the back of the watering can is visible, but the front cannot be seen. The second picture is angled to look directly down the spout of the watering can; this picture provides information about the front of the can that was not visible in the first photograph, but now the handle cannot be seen. The height of the watering can cannot be discerned from the bird's eye view of the third picture. The fourth picture is the obvious choice for the catalog; the watering can's height, top, spout, and handle are all discernible in this image. The motivation of PCA is similar; it can project data in a high-dimensional space to a lower dimensional space such that it retains as much of the variance as possible. PCA rotates the dataset to align with its principal components to maximize the variance contained within the first several principal components. Assume that we have the dataset that is plotted in the following screenshot:

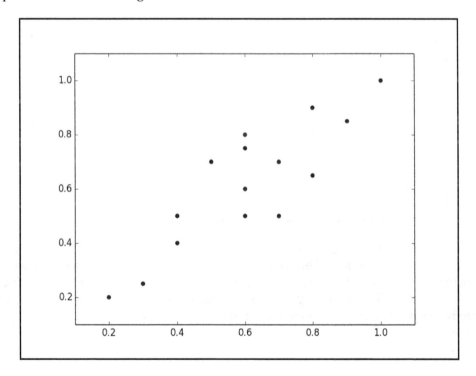

The instances approximately form a long, thin ellipse stretching from the origin to the top-right corner of the plot. To reduce the dimensions of this dataset, we must project the points onto a line. The following are two lines that the data can be projected onto. Along which line do the instances vary the most?

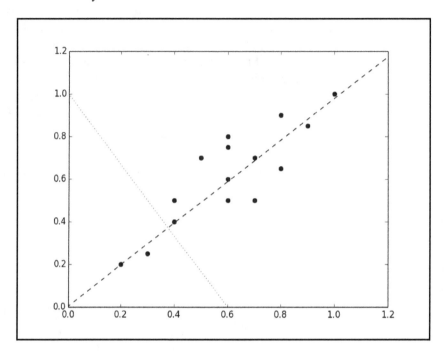

The instances vary more along the dashed line than the dotted line. In fact, the dashed line is the first principal component. The second principal component must be orthogonal to the first principal component; that is, it must be statistically independent of the first principal component. In a two-dimensional space, the first and second principal components will appear to be perpendicular, as shown in the following screenshot:

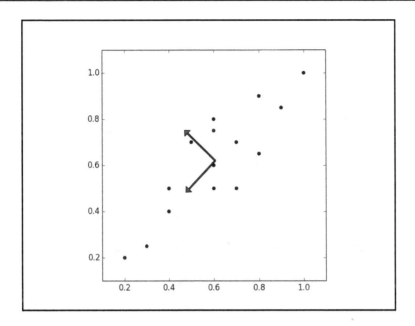

Each subsequent principal component preserves the maximum amount of the remaining variance; the only constraint is that it must be orthogonal to the other principal components. Now assume that the dataset is three-dimensional. The scatter plot of the previous points looks like a flat disc that has been rotated slightly about one of the axes.

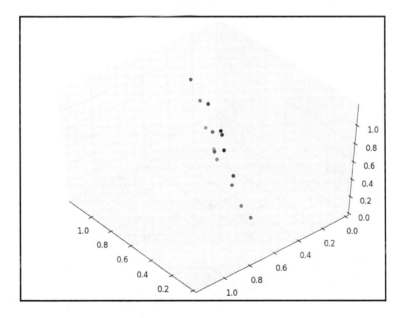

The points can be rotated and translated such that the tilted disk lies almost exactly in two dimensions. The points now form an ellipse; the third dimension contains almost no variance and can be discarded. PCA is most useful when the variance in a dataset is distributed unevenly across the dimensions. Consider a three-dimensional dataset with a spherical convex hull. PCA cannot be used effectively with this dataset because there is equal variance in each dimension; none of the dimensions can be discarded without losing a significant amount of information. It is easy to visually identify the principal components of datasets with only two or three dimensions. In the next section, we will discuss how to calculate the principal components of high-dimensional data.

Variance, covariance, and covariance matrices

There are several terms that we must define before discussing how PCA works. Recall that variance is a measure of how spread out a set of values is. Variance is calculated as the average of the squared differences of the values and the mean of the values, per the following equation:

$$s^2 = \frac{\sum_{i=1}^{n}(X_i - \bar{X})^2}{n-1}$$

Covariance is a measure of how much two variables change together; it is a measure of the strength of the correlation between two sets of variables. If the covariance of two variables is zero, the variables are uncorrelated. Note that uncorrelated variables are not necessarily independent, as correlation is only a measure of linear dependence. The covariance of two variables is calculated using the following equation:

$$cov(X, Y) = \frac{\sum_{i=1}^{n}(X_i - \bar{x})(Y_i - \bar{y})}{n-1}$$

If the covariance is non-zero, the sign indicates whether the variables are positively or negatively correlated. When two variables are positively correlated, one increases as the other increases. One variable decreases relative to its mean as the other variable increases relative to its mean when variables are negatively correlated. A **covariance matrix** describes the covariances between each pair of dimensions in a dataset. The element *(i, j)* indicates the covariance of the ith and j^{th} dimensions of the data. For example, a covariance matrix for a set of three-dimensional data is given by the following matrix:

$$C = \begin{bmatrix} cov(x_1, x_1) & cov(x_1, x_2) & cov(x_1, x_3) \\ cov(x_2, x_1) & cov(x_2, x_2) & cov(x_2, x_3) \\ cov(x_3, x_1) & cov(x_3, x_2) & cov(x_3, x_3) \end{bmatrix}$$

Let's calculate the covariance matrix for the following dataset:

v1	v2	v3
2	0	−1.4
2.2	0.2	−1.5
2.4	0.1	−1
1.9	0	−1.2

The means of the variables are 2.125, 0.075, and -1.275. We can then calculate the covariances of each pair of variables to produce the following covariance matrix:

$$C = \begin{bmatrix} 2.92 & 3.16 & 2.95 & 2.67 \\ 3.16 & 3.43 & 3.175 & 2.885 \\ 2.95 & 3.175 & 3.01 & 2.705 \\ 2.67 & 2.885 & 2.705 & 2.443 \end{bmatrix}$$

We can verify our calculations using NumPy:

```
# In[1]:
import numpy as np

X = np.array([
  [2, 0, -1.4],
  [2.2, 0.2, -1.5],
  [2.4, 0.1, -1],
  [1.9, 0, -1.2]
])
print(np.cov(X).T)

# Out[1]:
[[ 2.92        3.16        2.95        2.67       ]
 [ 3.16        3.43        3.175       2.885      ]
 [ 2.95        3.175       3.01        2.705      ]
 [ 2.67        2.885       2.705       2.44333333]]
```

Eigenvectors and eigenvalues

Recall that a vector is described by a direction and a magnitude, or length. An eigenvector of a matrix is a non-zero vector that satisfies the following equation:

$$A\vec{v} = \lambda\vec{v}$$

Here, $\vec{v}$ is an eigenvector, A is a square matrix, and λ is a scalar called an **eigenvalue**. The direction of an eigenvector remains the same after it has been transformed by A; only its magnitude changes, as indicated by the eigenvalue. That is, multiplying a matrix by one of its eigenvectors is equal to scaling the eigenvector. The prefix eigen is the German word for "belonging to' or "peculiar to"; the eigenvectors of a matrix are the vectors that "belong to" and characterize the structure of the data.

Eigenvectors and eigenvalues are can only be derived from square matrices, and not all square matrices have eigenvectors or eigenvalues. If a matrix does have eigenvectors and eigenvalues, it will have a pair for each of its dimensions. The principal components of a matrix are the eigenvectors of its covariance matrix, ordered by their corresponding eigenvalues. The eigenvector with the greatest eigenvalue is the first principal component; the second principal component is the eigenvector with the second greatest eigenvalue, and so on.

Let's calculate the eigenvectors and eigenvalues of the following matrix:

$$A = \begin{bmatrix} 1 & -2 \\ 2 & -3 \end{bmatrix}$$

Recall that the product of A and any eigenvector of A must be equal to the eigenvector multiplied by its eigenvalue. We will begin by finding the eigenvalues, which we can find using the characteristic equation:

$$(A - \lambda I)\,\vec{v} = 0$$

$$|A - \lambda * I| = \left| \begin{bmatrix} 1 & -2 \\ 2 & -3 \end{bmatrix} - \begin{bmatrix} \lambda & 0 \\ 0 & \lambda \end{bmatrix} \right| = 0$$

The characteristic equation states that the determinant of the matrix that is the difference between the data matrix and the product of the identity matrix and an eigenvalue is zero.

$$\left| \begin{bmatrix} 1-\lambda & -2 \\ 2 & -3-\lambda \end{bmatrix} \right| = (\lambda+1)(\lambda+1) = 0$$

$$(A - \lambda I)\vec{v} = 0$$

Substituting our values for A produces the following:

$$\left(\begin{bmatrix} 1 & -2 \\ 2 & -3 \end{bmatrix} - \begin{bmatrix} \lambda & 0 \\ 0 & \lambda \end{bmatrix} \right) \vec{v} = \begin{bmatrix} 1-\lambda & -2 \\ 2 & -3-\lambda \end{bmatrix} \vec{v} = \begin{bmatrix} 1-\lambda & -2 \\ 2 & -3-\lambda \end{bmatrix} \begin{bmatrix} v_{1,1} \\ v_{1,2} \end{bmatrix} = 0$$

We can then substitute in our first eigenvalue to solve for the eigenvectors.

$$\begin{bmatrix} 1-(-1) & -2 \\ 2 & -3-(-1) \end{bmatrix} \begin{bmatrix} v_{1,1} \\ v_{1,2} \end{bmatrix} = \begin{bmatrix} 2 & -2 \\ 2 & -2 \end{bmatrix} \begin{bmatrix} v_{1,1} \\ v_{1,2} \end{bmatrix} = 0$$

The preceding steps can be rewritten as a system of equations:

$$\begin{cases} 2v_{1,1} + -(2v_{1,2}) = 0 \\ 2v_{1,1} + -(2v_{1,2}) = 0 \end{cases}$$

Any non-zero vector that satisfies the preceding equations, such as the following, can be used as the eigenvector:

$$\begin{bmatrix} 1 & -2 \\ 2 & -3 \end{bmatrix} \begin{bmatrix} 1 \\ 1 \end{bmatrix} = -1 \begin{bmatrix} 1 \\ 1 \end{bmatrix} = \begin{bmatrix} -1 \\ -1 \end{bmatrix}$$

PCA requires unit eigenvectors, or eigenvectors that have length equal to 1. We can normalize an eigenvector by dividing it by its norm, which is given by the following equation:

$$||x|| = \sqrt{x_1^2 + x_2^2 + \ldots + x_n^2}$$

The norm of our vector is equal to:

$$\left| \left| \begin{bmatrix} 1 \\ 1 \end{bmatrix} \right| \right| = \sqrt{1^2 + 1^2} = \sqrt{2}$$

This produces the following unit eigenvector:

$$\begin{bmatrix} 1 \\ 1 \end{bmatrix} / \sqrt{2} = \begin{bmatrix} 0.707 \\ 0.707 \end{bmatrix}$$

We can verify that our solutions for the eigenvectors are correct using NumPy. The `eig` function returns a tuple of the eigenvalues and the eigenvectors:

```
# In[1]:
import numpy as np
w, v = np.linalg.eig(np.array([[1, -2], [2, -3]]))
print(w)
print(v)

# Out[1]:
[-0.99999998 -1.00000002]
[[ 0.70710678  0.70710678]
 [ 0.70710678  0.70710678]]
```

Performing PCA

Let's use PCA to reduce the following two-dimensional dataset to one dimension:

x1	x2
0.9	1
2.4	2.6
1.2	1.7
0.5	0.7
0.3	0.7
1.8	1.4
0.5	0.6
0.3	0.6
2.5	2.6
1.3	1.1

The first step of PCA is to subtract the mean of each explanatory variable from each observation:

x1	x2
0.9 - 1.17 = -0.27	1 - 1.3 = -0.3
2.4 - 1.17 = 1.23	2.6 - 1.3 = 1.3
1.2 - 1.17 = 0.03	1.7 - 1.3 = 0.4
0.5 - 1.17 = -0.67	-0.7 - 1.3 = 0.6
0.3 - 1.17 = -0.87	-0.7 - 1.3 = 0.6
1.8 - 1.17 = 0.63	1.4 - 1.3 = 0.1
0.5 - 1.17 = -0.67	0.6 - 1.3 = -0.7
0.3 - 1.17 = -0.87	0.6 - 1.3 = -0.7
2.5 - 1.17 = 1.33	2.6 - 1.3 = 1.3
1.3 - 1.17 = 0.13	1.1 - 1.3 = -0.2

Next, we must calculate the principal components of the data. Recall that the principal components are the eigenvectors of the data's covariance matrix ordered by their eigenvalues. The principal components can be found using two different techniques. The first technique requires calculating the covariance matrix of the data. Since the covariance matrix will be a square, we can calculate the eigenvectors and eigenvalues using the approach described in the previous section. The second technique uses singular value decomposition of the data matrix to find the eigenvectors and the square roots of the eigenvalues of the covariance matrix. We will work through an example using the first technique, and then describe the second technique, which is used by scikit-learn's implementation of PCA. The following is the covariance matrix for the data:

$$C = \begin{bmatrix} 0.687 & 0.607 \\ 0.607 & 0.598 \end{bmatrix}$$

Using the technique described in the previous section, the eigenvalues are *1.250* and *0.034*. The following are the unit eigenvectors:

$$\begin{bmatrix} 0.732 & -0.681 \\ 0.681 & 0.733 \end{bmatrix}$$

Next we will project the data onto the principal components. The first eigenvector has the greatest eigenvalue and is the first principal component. We will build a transformation matrix in which each column of the matrix is the eigenvector for a principal component. If we were reducing a five-dimensional dataset to three dimensions, we would build a matrix with three columns. In this example, we will project our two-dimensional dataset onto one dimension, so we will use only the eigenvector for the first principal component. Finally, we will find the dot product of the data matrix and the transformation matrix. The following is the result of projecting our data onto the first principal component:

$$
\begin{bmatrix}
-0.27 & -0.3 \\
1.23 & 1.3 \\
0.03 & 0.4 \\
-0.67 & -0.6 \\
-0.87 & -0.6 \\
0.63 & 0.1 \\
-0.67 & -0.7 \\
-0.87 & -0.7 \\
1.33 & 1.3 \\
0.13 & -0.2
\end{bmatrix}
\begin{bmatrix}
0.733 \\
0.681
\end{bmatrix}
=
\begin{bmatrix}
-0.40 \\
1.79 \\
0.29 \\
-0.90 \\
-1.05 \\
0.53 \\
-0.97 \\
-1.11 \\
1.86 \\
-0.04
\end{bmatrix}
$$

Many implementations of PCA, including scikit-learn's, use singular value decomposition to calculate the eigenvectors and eigenvalues. SVD is given by the following equation:

$$X = U\Sigma V^T$$

The columns of U are called the left-singular vectors of the data matrix, the columns V of are its right singular vectors, and the diagonal entries of Σ are its singular values. While the singular vectors and values of a matrix are useful in some applications of signal processing and statistics, we are only interested in them as they relate to the eigenvectors and eigenvalues of the data matrix. Specifically, the left-singular vectors are the eigenvectors of the covariance matrix and the diagonal elements of Σ are the square roots of the eigenvalues of the covariance matrix. Calculating SVD is beyond the scope of this chapter; however, eigenvectors found using SVD should be similar to those derived from a covariance matrix.

Visualizing high-dimensional data with PCA

It is easy to discover patterns by visualizing data with two or three dimensions. A high-dimensional dataset cannot be represented graphically, but we can still gain some insights into its structure by reducing it to two or three principal components. Collected in 1936, Fisher's Iris dataset is a collection of fifty samples from each of three species of Iris: Iris setosa, Iris virginica, and Iris versicolor. The explanatory variables are measurements of the length and width of the petals and sepals of the flowers. The Iris dataset is commonly used to test classification models, and is included with scikit-learn. Let's reduce the iris dataset's four dimensions so that we can visualize it in two dimensions. First we load the built-in iris dataset and instantiate a PCA estimator. The PCA class takes the number of principal components to retain as a hyperparameter. Like the other estimators, PCA exposes a fit_transform method that returns the reduced data matrix. Finally, we assemble and plot the reduced data:

```
# In[1]:
import matplotlib.pyplot as plt
from sklearn.decomposition import PCA
from sklearn.datasets import load_iris

data = load_iris()
y = data.target
X = data.data
pca = PCA(n_components=2)
reduced_X = pca.fit_transform(X)

red_x, red_y = [], []
blue_x, blue_y = [], []
green_x, green_y = [], []
for i in range(len(reduced_X)):
    if y[i] == 0:
        red_x.append(reduced_X[i][0])
        red_y.append(reduced_X[i][1])
    elif y[i] == 1:
        blue_x.append(reduced_X[i][0])
        blue_y.append(reduced_X[i][1])
    else:
        green_x.append(reduced_X[i][0])
        green_y.append(reduced_X[i][1])
plt.scatter(red_x, red_y, c='r', marker='x')
plt.scatter(blue_x, blue_y, c='b', marker='D')
plt.scatter(green_x, green_y, c='g', marker='.')
plt.show()
```

The reduced instances are plotted in the following figure. Each of the dataset's three classes is indicated by its own marker style. From this two-dimensional view of the data, it is clear that one of the classes can be easily separated from the other two overlapping classes. It would be difficult to notice this structure without a graphical representation. This insight can inform our choice of classification model.

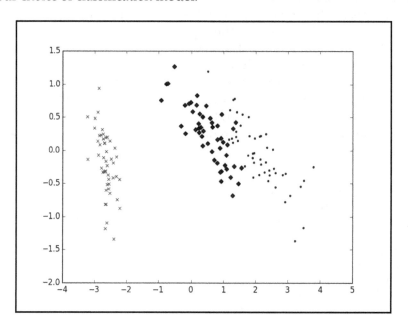

Face recognition with PCA

Now let's apply PCA to a face recognition problem. Face recognition is the supervised classification task of identifying a person from an image of his or her face. In this example, we will use a dataset called Our Database of Faces from AT&T Laboratories Cambridge. The dataset contains *10* images of each of *40* people. The images were created under different lighting conditions, and the subjects varied their facial expressions. The images are grayscale and in pixels. The following is an example image:

While these images are small, a feature vector that encodes the intensity of every pixel will have *10,304* dimensions. Training from such high-dimensional data could require many samples to avoid overfitting. Instead, we will use PCA to compactly represent the images in terms of a small number of principal components. We can reshape the matrix of pixel intensities for an image into a vector, and create a matrix of these vectors for all the training images. Each image is a linear combination of this dataset's principal components. In the context of face recognition, these principal components are called eigenfaces. The eigenfaces can be thought of as standardized components of faces. Each face in the dataset can be expressed as some combination of the eigenfaces, and can be approximated as a combination of the most important eigenfaces. We begin by loading the images into NumPy arrays and reshaping their pixel intensity matrices into vectors. We then standardize the data using the `scale` function. Recall that standardized data has zero mean and unit variance. It is important to standardize the data because PCA attempts to maximize the variances of the principal components; if the data is not standardized, PCA will be sensitive to the features' units and ranges:

```
# In[1]:
import os
import numpy as np
from sklearn.cross_validation import train_test_split
from sklearn.cross_validation import cross_val_score
from sklearn.preprocessing import scale
from sklearn.decomposition import PCA
from sklearn.linear_model import LogisticRegression
from sklearn.metrics import classification_report
from PIL import Image

X = []
y = []

for dirpath, _, filenames in os.walk('att-faces/orl_faces'):
    for filename in filenames:
        if filename[-3:] == 'pgm':
            img = Image.open(os.path.join(dirpath,
                filename)).convert('L')
            arr = np.array(img).reshape(10304).astype('float32') /
                255.
            X.append(arr)
            y.append(dirpath)

X = scale(X)
```

We then randomly split the images into training and test sets, and fit the PCA object on the training set:

```
# In[2]:
X_train, X_test, y_train, y_test = train_test_split(X, y)
pca = PCA(n_components=150)
```

We reduce all the instances to 150 dimensions and train a logistic regression classifier. The dataset contains 40 classes; scikit-learn automatically creates binary classifiers using the one-versus-all strategy behind the scenes. Finally, we evaluate the performance of the classifier using cross validation and a test set. The average per-class F1 Score of the classifier trained on the full data scored 0.94, but it required significantly more time to train and could be prohibitively slow in an application with more training instances:

```
# In[3]:
X_train_reduced = pca.fit_transform(X_train)
X_test_reduced = pca.transform(X_test)
print(X_train.shape)
print(X_train_reduced.shape)
classifier = LogisticRegression()
accuracies = cross_val_score(classifier, X_train_reduced,
    y_train)
print('Cross validation accuracy: %s' % np.mean(accuracies))
classifier.fit(X_train_reduced, y_train)
predictions = classifier.predict(X_test_reduced)
print(classification_report(y_test, predictions))

# Out[3]:
(300, 10304)
(300, 150)
Cross validation accuracy: 0.807660834984
```

	precision	recall	f1-score	support
att-faces/orl_faces/s1	0.50	1.00	0.67	1
att-faces/orl_faces/s10	1.00	1.00	1.00	3
att-faces/orl_faces/s11	1.00	0.67	0.80	3
att-faces/orl_faces/s12	1.00	1.00	1.00	5
att-faces/orl_faces/s13	0.00	0.00	0.00	0
att-faces/orl_faces/s14	1.00	1.00	1.00	4
att-faces/orl_faces/s16	1.00	1.00	1.00	2
att-faces/orl_faces/s17	0.67	1.00	0.80	2
att-faces/orl_faces/s18	1.00	1.00	1.00	2
att-faces/orl_faces/s19	0.83	1.00	0.91	5
att-faces/orl_faces/s2	0.33	1.00	0.50	1
att-faces/orl_faces/s20	1.00	1.00	1.00	2
att-faces/orl_faces/s21	1.00	1.00	1.00	2
att-faces/orl_faces/s22	1.00	1.00	1.00	1

att-faces/orl_faces/s23	0.67	1.00	0.80	2
att-faces/orl_faces/s24	1.00	1.00	1.00	3
att-faces/orl_faces/s25	1.00	1.00	1.00	2
att-faces/orl_faces/s26	1.00	1.00	1.00	3
att-faces/orl_faces/s27	1.00	1.00	1.00	1
att-faces/orl_faces/s28	1.00	0.50	0.67	4
att-faces/orl_faces/s29	1.00	1.00	1.00	5
att-faces/orl_faces/s3	1.00	1.00	1.00	3
att-faces/orl_faces/s30	1.00	0.67	0.80	3
att-faces/orl_faces/s31	0.75	1.00	0.86	3
att-faces/orl_faces/s32	1.00	1.00	1.00	3
att-faces/orl_faces/s34	1.00	0.83	0.91	6
att-faces/orl_faces/s35	0.50	0.33	0.40	3
att-faces/orl_faces/s36	1.00	1.00	1.00	3
att-faces/orl_faces/s37	1.00	0.75	0.86	4
att-faces/orl_faces/s38	1.00	1.00	1.00	3
att-faces/orl_faces/s39	1.00	1.00	1.00	2
att-faces/orl_faces/s4	1.00	0.75	0.86	4
att-faces/orl_faces/s40	0.00	0.00	0.00	0
att-faces/orl_faces/s5	1.00	0.67	0.80	3
att-faces/orl_faces/s6	1.00	1.00	1.00	1
att-faces/orl_faces/s7	1.00	1.00	1.00	3
att-faces/orl_faces/s8	1.00	1.00	1.00	2
att-faces/orl_faces/s9	1.00	1.00	1.00	1
avg / total	0.94	0.90	0.91	100

Summary

In this chapter, we examined the problem of dimensionality reduction. High-dimensional data suffers from the curse of dimensionality; estimators require many samples to be learned to generalize from high-dimensional data. We mitigated these problems using a technique called PCA, which reduces a high-dimensional, possibly correlated dataset to a lower dimensional set of linearly uncorrelated principal components by projecting the data onto a lower dimensional subspace. We used principal component analysis to visualize the four-dimensional iris dataset in two dimensions, and to build a face recognition system.

This chapter concludes the book. We have discussed a variety of models, learning algorithms, and performance measures, as well as their implementations in scikit-learn. In the first chapter, we described machine learning programs as those that learn from experience to improve their performance at a task. In the subsequent chapters, we worked through examples that demonstrated some of the most common experiences, tasks, and performance measures in machine learning. We regressed the prices of pizzas onto their diameters, and classified spam and ham text messages. We used principal component analysis for facial recognition, built a random forest to block banner advertisements, and used SVMs and ANNs for optical character recognition. I hope that you will be able to use scikit-learn and this book's examples to apply machine learning to your own experiences. Thank you for reading.

Index

www.ingramcontent.com/pod-product-compliance
Lightning Source LLC
Chambersburg PA
CBHW060539060326
40690CB00017B/3548

* 9 7 8 1 7 8 8 2 9 9 8 7 9 *